the OUTRAGEOUS Manager

Roger McAniff

McBliss & Associates

McBliss & Associates
302 1st Street West, Suite 203
Polson, MT 59860
Phone: (406) 883-3671
Fax: (406) 883-3672
email: roger@mcbliss.com

05 04 03 02 01 00 99   5 4 3 2 1
First printing, 1999

Typesetting and Interior Design by Michael Dougherty
Cover design by Laura Donovan

McAniff, Roger
        The Outrageous Manager: Managing the Basics, Leading
Change, Energizing Relationships, Mastering the Truth/Roger McAniff,—
1st ed.
        p. cm.
        Includes bibliographical references
        Preassigned LCCN. 98-96457
        ISBN 0-9666072-0-1
1. Management 2. Organizational change I. Title

HD38.2 M32 1998   658.4
                          QB198-956

This book is dedicated to my clients and colleagues and to all the outrageous people I have encountered on my journey.

Acknowledgements

No one writes a book alone. We are influenced by those we have read, our colleagues, our clients, our friends and countless others. It is impossible to thank everyone who has helped to shape this book and yet there are a few who have had a major influence who I would like to mention.

Kappie Bliss helped me to understand and to enjoy relationships and gave me the love and freedom to create and complete this book. She truly energizes relationships.

Jim Horan helped at every step along the way and initiated the articles on benchmarking, accountability, business models, failure to implement and political directness. He is a master of managing the basics and his gentle guidance gave me the courage to write my truth.

Jerry Hubbard taught, worked and played with me for many years and helped me explore the intricacies of mastering the truth.

Bernie Johansen explored and collaborated with me on large scale systems change and taught me the interplay between change and technology

Susie Kelley and Mike Wolfe developed countless teams with me and helped form my conclusions on developing effective teams.

Chris Totolis traveled the country with me for five years and helped me learn the basics, computer simulation, modeling, manufacturing and how to have fun.

Tom Luhmann traveled with me for a different five years and helped me learn marketing and economic development.

Deborah Grant taught me the intricacies of staffing and helped write the staffing articles.

Jeanne Anne Craig happily collaborated on working relationships and negotiation.

Laurinda Harmon introduced me to the power and joy of psychic energy.

Barb Greene helped me understand myself, the depths of life and all the dimensions of truth and commitment.

Charlie Seashore explored the intense feelings of change and the power of groups.

Will McWhinney shared his explorations of systems and reality. ■

Forward

Ihave always been mesmerized and fascinated by business. The business leaders I have worked with are the most creative, hard working and interesting people I know. They are all different and have their unique styles and approaches and their personal strengths and weaknesses. They share a passion for business and success and a commitment to give it their best shot. Hundreds of business leaders have hired me as their consultant over the past thirty years and they have become my mentors and teachers.

They have walked me through the maze of underground mine tunnels, into the guts of pulp and paper plants, around the acrid beds of burn wards, under the huge boiling vats of lead smelters, amidst the din of machinery shaping metal, above the carefully designed processes for mixing explosives, into the clean rooms of highly sophisticated and sensitive chemical processes, through the gigantic assembly plants for aircraft, around noisy electric power plants of all shapes and sizes, among countless offices and computer rooms and hundreds of other complex and fascinating places. They have shared their ideas, their knowledge, their hopes and dreams, their plans and goals, their problems and challenges, their fears, their frailty, their deep strength and eventually themselves.

When I first started in the consulting business, I was very bright, naive, arrogant, driven, curious and in awe of the leaders because of their power and position. The curiosity saved me and allowed me to learn and grow for the next thirty years. I am now humble, curious and still in awe of the business leaders. Today, the awe comes from their ability to continue and thrive in the face of uncertainty, adversity and seemingly overwhelming odds. My curiosity remains unabated.

Several years ago I went back to school into a doctoral program because I felt my consulting practice might not be grounded in the latest theories and I wanted to update my business education. While I greatly broadened my understanding of human beings and social interaction, I found (not surprisingly, in retrospect) that my business education had been first rate at the hands of the business leaders who I had been working with for years. Their theories, if they used any, were forged based on first hand experience and tested immediately under the most stressful of conditions.

I learned most from those business leaders who were open to change and succeeded, but I also learned a lot from those who made critical mistakes and failed. Many of the successful leaders had made past mistakes or suffered agonizing failures and learned from them to go on and become better and better at their trade. Every business leader has many stories about where they began, how they have progressed in business, learned their trade and become who they are today. Each story is unique and fascinating on its own. Since they are my mentors, my business success story is a compilation of all their stories and all their experiences.

Most of the business leaders I have worked with have a bias for action and use their pragmatic senses to guide their actions. As a consultant and teacher, I have biases for reflection, insight and creating models. Over the years, I have continually created and updated my models for business success. They have been tested, revised and updated quite often and they are always dynamic. I tried for many years to find or create the perfect model that would always work and have discovered that it does not exist. What does exist however is the accumulated wisdom that has been developed by the many leaders and elders who have shaped modern business. This wisdom is continually changing and growing as we learn and adapt to new business challenges and conditions. I would classify this wisdom in terms of principles and approaches rather than rules or prescriptions.

Native American beliefs say that we can come into wisdom in our fiftieth year. Having passed that milestone, I feel that perhaps I have accumulated enough business wisdom to share my journey and findings with others interested in the subject of business success. I do this with great humility and respect for those who have gone before, especially those who have had the foresight and courage to blaze the path of American business.

Wisdom is defined as accumulated philosophic or scientific learning, the ability to discern inner qualities and relationships, and insight or good sense. This book is organized around my basic philosophy that successful businesses manage the basics, change continuously, develop excellent working relationships, and master the truth.

Roger McAniff
Big Arm, Montana 1998

Contents

Introduction

Outrageous is defined as: exceeding the limits of what is usual; not conventional or matter of fact; and deficient in propriety. All of these definitions are qualities that managers need and will find in this book. Being outrageous is absolutely necessary to survive and thrive in business and organizations today. Playing it safe and being cautious and conservative will leave you in the dust.

Outrageous managers have four major qualities and abilities that serve them well and separate them from their peers. They manage the basics of their business. They understand and lead change efforts and actually get them implemented and working. They energize their working relationships and teams. And they are continually working to discover, speak and master the truth. This doesn't sound very outrageous until you look at these qualities a little deeper.

Most businesses and organizations I have worked with are looking for quick fixes, panaceas or magical answers to their present problems or situations. Almost none of those quick solutions work but we keep believing in them and trying the new fads because we don't want to fail and we don't want to stand still. We also know that the real problems are difficult and will take a lot of hard work to resolve. Over the years we have tried zero defects, job enrichment, quality circles, total quality, teams, outsourcing, re-engineering, systems, management by objectives, intricate performance measurement systems, 360 degree reviews, reorganizations and many other programs and directions. Each of them had some value and none of them solved the core business problems and led to excellent results.Outrageous managers have returned to the basics and concentrate on the three "P"s of planning, process (people) and performance. It's outrageous because it is simple, clear and centers around accountability and performance. No fads, no gimmicks, just clear plans, good process and a lot of attention to achieving performance. Everyone is held accountable and everyone performs. Almost achieving goals is unacceptable and dealt with immediately.

The second outrageous quality is leading change and actually getting it implemented. Countless change efforts have been initiated in most businesses and organizations and very few of them succeed. Change is normally poorly understood, top down and takes too long. Change is also normally managed rather than led and ignores all the key human factors that are necessary to make change succeed. We live in a world of continuous change and don't really know how to design and implement effective change.

Outrageous managers learn to understand and lead change efforts and actually achieve the results that were desired. They do this through understanding the levels and types of change necessary, continually developing their leadership skills and leading the appropriate processes for the types of change needed. They also continue to apply the basics and keep their eye firmly on the goals and objectives of the change efforts.

The chapter on leading change presents a model that summarizes 30 years of leading change. The model helps to differentiate simple change from transitional change and transformational change. Each of these require different processes and escalating levels of effort. Simple change is behavior oriented and can be designed and implemented with little discussion and minimal training. Transitional change is a systems change that requires extensive input, participation and processing to achieve the desired results. Transitional change also requires clear mental models of the new system (system is used in its broadest sense) and processing of the emotions involved in making the transition. Transformational change is the deepest change and takes the most effort and follows the most difficult path. Transformations are only made by choice and with the support of the participants. Transformation change also requires very creative and non-traditional processes to help the participants to see the new situation from outside their current reality.

The change model also differentiates among individual change, group change and organization change. The processes and complexity change as the number of people involved grows. Simple individual change is the easiest and most straightforward change process and organization transformation is the most difficult and complex process. It should be observed that while simple individual change is the easiest, it can be far from simple. All of us have gone through change processes and none of them have been simple. Outrageously leading change involves creative leadership, tenacity, a lot of energy, thorough understanding of the processes, time and commitment.

The third outrageous quality is energizing our working relationships and teams. Over 85% of the turnover in organizations is traced to failed working relationships, not performance issues. Work is essentially human and personal and we need to pay attention to our working relationships to help them work. This chapter of the book outlines models for successful working relationships and successful teams. Both are critical elements for reaching goals and achieving results. Yet both are normally ignored by organizations until they are at a crisis stage.

Energizing relationships means that we not only perform the actions necessary to make the relationships work, we make everyone in the relationship or on the team better at what they do. The great team players not only perform at a high level, they raise the level of everyone around them. They bring a lot of energy to what they do and share it with others. Each of their working relationships appears to be special and the people they work with want to be around them and work with them. This is not charisma, it is the quality of being yourself, bringing your passion and sharing it with others.

Propriety has become prevalent in our businesses and organizations. We must be careful of what we say, we don't want to offend anyone or hurt their feelings and we need to obfuscate the truth. We are also afraid of taking risks, making mistakes, appearing foolish, stepping out of the box, being different and disagreeing with the established norms and the dominant groups. This has become a disease to the point of becoming a critical epidemic. Double speak, half truths, political correctness, weasel wording, group think, and hundreds of other games have taken the place of straight talk, honesty and truth.

Outrageous managers ferret out and speak the truth. This is probably the most outrageous behavior of the outrageous manager and that is really scary. A common misconception is that good process in a business or organization means political correctness and touchy feely approaches to business. No Way! Good process is about effective ways of staying creative and getting results. Good process is based on knowing and speaking the truth—yes all of it—even when it is apparently bad news and may hurt us.

Discovering and speaking the truth is not easy. It takes diligence and work to discover the truth and a lot of courage to speak it. It also takes self knowledge and reflection. The truth is not always rational or even emotional. In many situations we need access to our intuition and inner knowing to ferret out the truth. Taking the time to reflect and check in with ourselves is part of the process. Doing that in business is outrageous.

Mastery is not a simple process or a linear path. Mastering the truth is a lifelong commitment to understanding ourselves at deeper and deeper levels and then sharing that path with others. Mastery is the path to understanding and wisdom and defines the journey that leads to long term success for ourselves, our relationships and our organizations. ■

Chapter 1:
Managing
The Basics

*T*he business approach for several decades was to try to break situations down into their component parts. Today, the approach is to take the systems or overall view so that we don't optimize parts of the business at the expense of the whole. Integrating all the parts into a cohesive and comprehensive whole system is a necessary component of business success.

Planning is normally the first step to business success. Planning includes the shared vision, mission, objectives, strategies, values, culture and plans of the business; and organizing the business to achieve the defined plans. Planning helps us define where we are going or want to go and how to get there. It sets the overall direction and tone for the business and provides the criteria for ongoing decision making. Planning can be simple and straightforward or very complicated and difficult. For most businesses, simple and easy to use plans that will actually be used to guide the business and focus the efforts of the management and staff are suggested.

The process element of business acknowledges that the transactions of business are conducted by people and that the quality of the business relationships are a key element of business success. Process includes how the business members relate to each other, their customers, their environment and their stakeholders. These working relationships encompass processes for communication, decision making, learning, development, healthy conflict, and ethics. Process is about how we conduct business and how we encourage and develop creativity, teamwork, intuition, change and other human qualities. Those subjects are addressed in later chapters in this book.

Performance is the last key element of business success and is certainly equally important with planning and process. Performance includes measuring, assessing and achieving the defined business plans; and the decisions and actions that drive operating, market, technical and financial performance. Performance is achieved through the daily decisions and actions of the managers and staff of the business and is the short term focus that drives each of the functional areas of the business.

Outrageous managers achieve outrageous results. They don't actually do anything that out of the ordinary. They just do everything they are supposed to do and they do it very well. They also work very hard, are passionate about what they do and spread their enthusiasm and dedication to others. Some of their characteristics are defined below.

Outrageous managers get things done. They accomplish defined goals and objectives with the resources available. They ship products, make sales, obtain loans, design products, perform services, make things, build things, move people or goods, develop software, operate systems, find resources, and do the thousands of tasks and functions that constitute doing business. Their emphasis is on keeping the business going and growing. The ingredients are action and results. They are results driven and continually in action.

Outrageous managers use resources wisely. They clearly establish what they need and then find a way to get them. They get the materials, computers, people, budgets, financing, designs, equipment, machinery, support and other resources necessary to do the job. They use the resources to reach their goals within established costs. They continually monitor what is being spent and what else is needed.

Outrageous managers work well with and through others. They plan, staff, organize, coordinate, monitor, measure, motivate, reward, and control the people and their actions to accomplish their goals. They work with executives, other managers, employees, suppliers, customers, bankers, investors, engineers, lawyers, accountants, sales and marketing, research and many others to get their work done. Managers spend most of their work time communicating with others in person, on the phone, in writing, via e-mail or in meetings. Communication occupies about 90% of their time and they do it well.

Outrageous managers make those around them better. They motivate, inspire, coach, instruct, encourage, discipline, push, chide, mentor, inform, guide or do whatever is necessary to continually improve how their superiors, peers and employees perform. Their own work habits and accomplishments tend to pull others along to work at higher levels.

Outrageous managers exude accountability. They set very clear measures of what is necessary to get the job done, monitor performance continually, hold everyone accountable for achieving their results and deal immediately with unacceptable performance. They create an environment of achievement and continually find new ways to keep that environment exciting and compelling.

Outrageous managers are continually learning and growing in their profession, their company, their function and their management skills. They emphasize learning for themselves and for those around them. Outrageous managers manage the basics and achieve outrageous results. ■

The Three "P"s To Excellent Business Results

An engineering firm defines a very small market niche, does their job very well and works well with each other and their clients. They fail due to poor planning.

A division of a Fortune 500 company develops an excellent team to enter a new market with an aggressive plan. They don't execute and pay attention to the details and they fail.

A large grocery company has an excellent plan and performs well but can't communicate and becomes unable to change and grow. They continually lose market share.

There are no pat answers, formulas or shortcuts to business success. After 30 years of business consulting and teaching, I have watched fads and philosophies come and go and what remains are the basics. Successful businesses have a clear plan, do it well and work well together. A business model that has worked well for me is the three P's. The three P's represent the three key elements of business success: Planning, Process and Performance. Mastering and integrating these three elements is the key to success.

Planning includes the shared vision, mission, objectives, strategies, values, culture and plans of the business; and organizing the business to achieve the defined plans. Planning also looks at how your business changes and how to manage that change.

Planning builds on success, solves critical problems and defines directions and strategies for the business.

Process includes how the business members relate to each other, their customers, their environment and their stakeholders. These working relationships encompass processes for communication, decision making, learning, development, healthy conflict, and ethics. Process also includes the methods used to manage and accomplish the business and get things done. Business processes are the core of how people act in the business and what they actually do and accomplish. The processes energize or stifle business growth.

Performance includes measuring, assessing and achieving the defined business plans; and the decisions and actions that drive operating, market, technical and financial results. Performance is the implementation of the plans and processes and defines the quantifiable actions that produce results. Failure to implement is the single largest cause of business failures. Developing a high performance atmosphere and achieving early success can go a long way to achieving continued business success

These three elements interact with each other to form an integrated dynamic system. The center of that system is the management that leads and integrates the three elements and ensures that results are achieved. Without management providing the positive energy, leadership and integration of the key elements, no business can succeed for very long. This can be a daunting challenge to those running a business. Happily, a good plan with a shared vision can provide a lot of positive energy; effective process on an executive team can provide shared leadership; and the integration does not have to come from one person. Paying attention to the three P's is the key. Finding the balance is the challenge. ■

Discussion Questions:

1. Which of the three P's is *your* strength? Which is *your* challenge?

2. How do *you* integrate the three? What internal and external resources are available?

Outrageous Managers balance the three "P"s.

Business Basics Checklist

*T*his checklist will give you an overview of how you are doing on the basics. Try it!

Planning:

- ☐ Do you have a clear and effective business plan? Is it used to focus action?
- ☐ Do you understand your success factors? Are you building on them?
- ☐ Have you defined your critical problems? Are you solving them?
- ☐ Have you defined what business you are in? From the customers' perspective?
- ☐ Does your customer drive your business?
- ☐ Are you organized for success? Does your organization fit your strategy?
- ☐ Are your strategies clear and used? Are they working?
- ☐ Would you buy your business today? Why not?

Process:

- ☐ Are your processes (such as teams and communication) tied to business goals and results?

- [ ] Do your working relationships support your business? Do you pay attention to them?
- [ ] Is your business innovative? Does it embrace change? Are you willing to change?
- [ ] Does your management team deal with the tough issues? Ask the hard questions?
- [ ] Do you have the necessary leaders to succeed? Are they managing or leading?
- [ ] Have you become bureaucratic? Do control and fear dominate your decisions?
- [ ] Can your employees share bad news? Do you hide negative data and information?
- [ ] Do you have the best people and the right people to succeed? Any non-performers?

Performance:

- [ ] Do you provide excellent customer service? Customer satisfaction? Do you know?
- [ ] Are you providing excellent products or services? Top quality? How do you know?
- [ ] Is your income statement healthy? Revenues? Expenses? Overhead? GandA? Controls?
- [ ] Is your financial house in order? Capital? Working capital? Debt? Cash?
- [ ] Do you effectively measure performance? Tied to business plan? Measuring the right factors? Easy to measure? Reported and checked often? Follow up on exceptions?
- [ ] Are your budgets a game or a valuable tool? Tied to business plan? Follow up?
- [ ] Have you benchmarked your business? Shared and followed up the results?
- [ ] Are your business processes current and supporting excellent results? Archaic?

☐ Are you using current, beneficial and appropriate technology? Too little? Too much?

☐ Do you perform effective market research? Do you use it to drive market decisions?

☐ Do you have an effective marketing plan? Is it generating sales?

☐ Are your plans being implemented? What are the blocks? Who is being protected? ■

Discussion Questions:

1. Which of these questions identifies a critical area limiting your performance? What will you do about it?

2. Who is holding your organization back? Is it you? What action will you take?

Outrageous Managers ask tough questions.

Business Planning

A *high technology company prepares an elaborate plan for their investors and bankers to finance the company. They see the plan as a painful exercise and a waste of time. They don't believe in it, don't follow the plan, and fail.*

A Fortune 500 company hires a major consulting firm to develop their strategic plan and position them for future growth. The plan is very elaborate and lengthy and the company doesn't really buy into it. The plan gathers dust on a book shelf.

A start-up company prepares their business plan based on what they have done in the past and what they think they should do now. They have no energy to implement the plan and they fail.

A radio company prepares a business plan in a couple of hours that summarizes their vision, mission, objectives, strategies and plans. They use it with their advisors, bankers and employees to get clear on their direction and to agree on how to proceed. Their business thrives and grows.

Business plans are not an exercise. Most business plans look like a computer dump with lots of pages of financials and projections. The financials and budgets are not business plans, they are the tools to implement well thought out and agreed upon plans.

Effective business plans are an opportunity to express ourselves through our business. Detailed plans and programs are the guides to implement our vision and mission. Business plans energize the business and provide the focus to keep it on track. Business plans are the roadmaps that define the journey we are undertaking and where we would like to end up. Business plans integrate the personal and professional and link us to our customers and communities.

The One Page Business Plan(tm) helps businesses to focus their thoughts and ideas and create effective business plans on one page. The key elements are the:

1. **Vision**. Describe your idea or business in a manner that captures the passion of the idea. The vision statement is YOUR statement of what you want to do and will do.

2. **Mission**. Describe why customers will buy from you and how you will connect to your customers and community.

3. **Objectives**. Describe specifically what you will accomplish this year and how you define success. What do you want to celebrate New Years Eve?

4. **Strategies**. Describe your overall approach and methodology and set the direction for achieving your goals. What path will you follow?

5. **Plans**. Describe the specific actions you will take to accomplish the objectives and follow the strategies. Plans assign accountability and deadlines.

Business plans are not optional. Create your plan and get your business on track. ∎

Discussion Questions:

1. Do you know where you are going? How you will get there?

2. Does your business plan express your passion? Why not?

Outrageous Managers summarize their business plans on one page.

Build On Success

A consulting firm continues to define itself as a process firm and to market its abilities that it thinks clients should need. It overlooks its wisdom and business skills and what clients actually want and need and fails to generate business.

A major manufacturer sees itself as a technology firm that leads its field in technical excellence. It invests in more technology and ignores its marketing strength. It declines.

A restaurant company recognizes its excellence in starting up and growing new or failing businesses. It succeeds based on buying and selling restaurants.

One of the key criteria for selecting a good strategy is to determine whether the strategy builds on your critical success factors. While most of us are very good at defining problems, defining the keys to our success is more elusive. It is also very important.

Your success factors are the one or two critical reasons why you have experienced success to date. The reason(s) could be technical, financial, market position, leadership, a unique niche, persistence, low cost, outstanding quality, location, reputation, or many others. These factors clearly define your edge, your reason for continuing in business and the keys to ongoing success. They are based on internal strengths or external opportunities and are unique to your business. If you have defined more than two critical success factors, then you aren't yet to the core of what makes you succeed. You may have lots of strengths and advantages and yet experience shows that there are not more than two critical factors that really drive all the other strengths and advantages. Don't stop until you find them.

How do we define these factors? Here are a few questions and clues that may help:

1. List all your strengths. Don't be shy, claim them if you have them.

2. List all your opportunities and your reasons for pursuing them.

3. List major past successes. What conditions were present when they occurred?

4. Ask your customers why they deal with you. Yes, they will tell you

5. Ask your competitors what they think your advantage is. Yes, they will also tell you.

6. If you are an entrepreneur or new company, look at your individual factors in the past.

7. Now, put all the lists together and start to look for similarities–what factors continue to appear? What factors lead to the other factors?

8. Continue analyzing the lists with brutal honesty until you can define the one or two critical factors that drive all the others and are your real keys to success.

9. If you are not sure or not clear, get help in the analytical phase

10. Clearly write the one or two critical success factors. One line each.

11. Edit until you resonate with the written findings.

Once you have defined your critical success factors, include them in your strategic plan and use them to evaluate and select your strategies. Strategies that build on your success lead to more success and excellent business results. ■

Discussion Questions:

1. What have been the keys to your success? Are you sure?

2. How are you leveraging that success?

Outrageous Managers build on their past successes.

Critical Problems

We've all been to the doctor and had our temperature, blood pressure, and vital signs checked to define the symptoms of what's wrong. The doctor then looks deeper to see what might be causing the symptoms. The doctor may give us some aspirin or medicines to alleviate the symptoms, but the goal is to solve the real problem and make us well.

Businesses are no different. Sometimes our businesses are not doing well and there may be many symptoms of what is wrong. Putting band aids on the symptoms will usually not solve the core problem(s) that are causing the business to perform poorly. In our day-to- day actions, we rarely have the time or resources to look carefully at what might really be wrong, so we solve the problems that are in front of us. The strategic or business planning process is where we need to take the time and look at all the symptoms of what might be wrong with the business and define the root or critical problems that must be addressed. I call them critical problems because they threaten the survivability of the business. They are root problems because they are the root cause of the other problems and symptoms.

Most of us have gone through the exercises of defining the strengths and weaknesses and the threats and opportunities of the business. We have also scanned the environment to see what new factors may be affecting us. These are useful exercises and necessary to get the process rolling. One of the most important steps to an effective plan starts after the weaknesses and threats have been defined. We now look at all the inputs and define the root and critical problems that are behind all the weaknesses and threats.

There are usually only one or two critical problems that face a business at a given time. In rare cases I have seen three. If you have defined more than that, you are probably not down to the root causes and critical problems. To get to that level:

1. List all the weaknesses that you can define for the business.

2. List all the threats that appear from the environment, competitors or other areas.

3. Scan the lists and create a new list of factors that affect the survival of the business.

4. Now try to define which of these are the causes of the others–that is, which factors lead the others to occur.

5. Stay with this until you get down to the one or two factors that are the root causes of all the others.

6. If you have trouble with this, pair off two remaining factors and ask which comes first or which might be the cause of the other. As you keep doing this with pairs of factors, the root causes will become clear.

7. As a last check, look at the final one or two factors and ask whether these are the issues that truly need to be solved to move the business along.

Solving the problems is not normally as difficult as defining which are the critical problems that we need to solve. Find them, and then solve them. Use them to guide your strategy. ■

Discussion Questions:

1. What are your critical problems? Are you sure?

2. What is the one recurring problem that holds you back from the next step? What is the root cause of that problem?

Outrageous Managers get to the root of critical problems and solve them.

Business Culture as a Strategy Tool

*T*he new CEO of a national company embarks on a bold plan to revitalize the company but fears that the culture can't support the new direction. He alienates the staff and fails.

The head of a major state agency defines a bold strategy that will reshape the culture of the agency and improve government performance. The plan loses steam and dies.

Culture is a strategic factor in the success of our businesses and yet it is still poorly understood and used. Business culture is defined as the basic assumptions, beliefs, artifacts, and values that are: shared over time by the people in a business; used to create meaning for the managers and employees; and drive the decisions and actions of the business. Culture is normally an unseen force inherent in the decisions and actions of the managers and employees, not a conscious force that is deliberated during those decisions and actions.

As an unseen force, it takes some effort to define it for your business and understand its effects on your business. We don't want to do that very often so it's best to look at culture when you are developing or reviewing your strategic plan. The use of business culture in the planning process is quite simple. Strategies that are consistent with your culture can work and those that are inconsistent will not work. So each proposed strategy needs to be put to the culture test–is it consistent? For new businesses, the question can be asked a different way. What culture do I need to develop to support the selected strategies? Once a culture has developed and grown, it is very difficult to change. Culture change should not be taken on except in very drastic circumstances.

So, how do we define the existing culture so that we can test our strategies? A few clues:

- List five to ten specific major decisions or actions that have happened in the past year.

- Start a process to ask what drove those decisions or actions. List specific reasons.

- Analyze what assumptions or beliefs might be inherent in the reasons or actions.

- See what beliefs or assumptions consistently show up in each decision or action.

- Be careful not to prejudge the outcomes. The truth is important to understand.

- Ask others who were not part of the decisions or actions to analyze the same list.

- If the business is in one locale, check with others on how they define the local culture.

- Ask a cross section of managers and employees to define their key values and beliefs.

- Put all the inputs together in writing and see what trends and common factors consistently appear. Those are probably the factors that define your business culture.

- Write a short and clear statement of the culture and get feedback from your staff.

- Finalize a statement to use as a test of proposed strategies.

Culture can be a very useful tool to check on the viability of proposed strategies. Like success factors, we want to develop and nourish positive cultural factors. ∎

Discussion Questions:

1. What practices or actions continue to occur, even after you have decided to change them? Why does this happen?

2. How can your culture work for you?

Outrageous Managers develop strategies that are consistent with their business cultures.

Organizing For Success

A large manufacturing company designed a new strategic direction and plan but left the old organization in place. They failed to generate momentum for the new plan.

Another large manufacturer spread their technical and research groups over several subsidiaries. The groups couldn't cooperate and new product development took too long.

A large engineering firm needed to generate new products and markets due to major changes in their traditional markets. They put the managers of their old divisions in charge of the new programs and all the new programs failed.

Company reorganizations are a frequent business occurrence. Successful reorganizations are quite infrequent. There are several key reasons for this:

- Reorganizations need to be done as part of implementing a new strategic plan.

- Reorganizations are a major change and require energy and leadership to implement.

- New directions and plans require leaders who are passionate about the changes.

- Reorganizations usually try to fit new programs into old ways of doing business.

- Reorganizations usually just reshuffle existing managers and workers into new "slots".

- Reorganizations are designed to control new programs rather than energize them.

The basic problem is that we try to go in new directions using the same thinking, people and processes that were used in the organization we are trying to change. Assuming that we are reorganizing because the old organization and direction were not working, then it follows that we need more than reshuffling. We need a new approach. Some suggestions for your new approach include:

- Have your strategies drive your projects and organization.

- Use the vision, mission and core values as the unifying forces to stay focused.

- Make the people with the energy around new ideas and directions responsible for them.

- Organize by responsibility centers instead of functions.

- Define linkages through relationships rather than lines and boxes.

- Have fluid organizations where key people can lead in areas where they are capable.

- Emphasize accountability and results rather than authority and chain of command.

- Use leadership to drive projects and influence to get support.

- Evaluate success frequently, measuring actions and results rather than words and reports.

- Make meetings voluntary where people choose to come based on interest and input.

- Keep organizations dynamic so they don't bog down in authority and control.

- Use task teams with a very limited life span.

- Share leadership where all the people involved can bring new ideas and approaches.

- Make sure your customer is included in the organization in a key place.

Reorganization is an integral part of the implementation of any planning process. Do it carefully and creatively and try concentrating on how you will energize new directions. ■

Discussion Questions:

1. Do you have the leadership, passion and energy you need to implement new directions?

2. How does your customer participate in your organization? Are you committed to hearing their input and serving their needs?

Outrageous Managers organize to serve their customers.

Putting Your Business Plan Into Action

Putting your business plan into action is the most important planning step because the actions deliver the results you wanted when you started the process. A few suggestions for uses of the plan are summarized below:

1. Use it to talk with your banker about financing. Sharing your plan with your banker will get you useful feedback and lead to improved banker relations.

2. Use your business plan to focus discussions with present or potential investors. The plan shows what you intend to do and how you will make it happen. Combined with your enthusiasm and commitment, the plan will help get and keep investors.

3. Convert the plan into budgets. Putting the plan into action requires quantifying the plans and objectives and getting the resources into place to support implementation. This is the process of budgeting. Don't be afraid of it! Budgets help define the resources we need and provide the measures that keep us on track.

4. Implementing the plan is the vital next step. More companies fail because of "Failure To

Implement" than for any other reason. Implementation is the process of using the goals, plans, measures and other tools that we have defined and making sure that the actions take place. Everyone must be held accountable for meeting their goals.

5. Make copies for everyone and have them post it on the wall of their office. Plans need to be communicated and understood to help drive the necessary decisions and actions that will lead to success. Certainly, all your managers and employees should have a copy of your plan and you may want to share it with advisors, bankers, accountants, suppliers, key customers, and key community members. Share it with anyone who could help your business succeed.

6. Review it at team and company meetings and get some energy going around it. Implementing the plan means paying attention to it. Don't let it sit on a shelf. Your business plan is a working document that will work for you if you continually use it to remind your team and your employees about where you are going and how you will get there.

7. Use it as a decision making tool. Managers make decisions on the fly every day. The business plan is the guide to make those decisions. The strategies, objectives and plans are very clear guides to where resources should be used and what the priorities should be. The vision and mission are more general guides that help determine the overall direction and the values and principles that apply. The plan as a whole is the prime decision making document that should be checked on every key business decision.

Useful plans drive decisions and actions and get everyone working toward the same goals. Decisions and actions that help implement the plan are positive and support the success of the company. Decisions and actions that go in different directions significantly reduce the probable success of the business. Make sure that your business plan is a working document that is put into action. ■

Discussion Questions:

1. What are the last three uses you made of your business plan? When?

2. Is your business plan used in your decision making process? Does everyone use it?

Outrageous Managers put their business plans into action.

Strategic Marketing

A *major electric utility company defined their customers as those people within their legally defined monopolistic service area. They failed to see the threats to their business from competing energy sources and also the opportunities to expand into related areas.*

A start up company was well financed and defined excellent promotion materials but failed to target their efforts and define their customers. They failed.

A major state agency spends millions of public dollars every year designing, maintaining and constructing roads and transportation systems. They isolated their decision processes from their customers and lost public support and funding.

Our vision for our business defines the business from our point of view. Turning that vision into a mission and a successful business involves defining the business from the customer's point of view. It seems that most businesses, whether public, private or non-profit, continually struggle with this marketing aspect of their business strategy. The crucial questions that must be asked are not easy and the answers can change over time. From a marketing perspective, the crucial questions include:

- What business are we in? From the customers perspective?

- Who are the customers? Would they know us as a supplier? Who pays for our products or services?

- Why do customers buy from us? How would they define the reasons?

Unless we can answer these questions, we can't really develop our business mission or strategic plan. We all know this and yet we struggle with the answers because we get locked into the way it has always been or the way we want it to be. It's actually much easier to answer these questions for someone else's business than for our own. For example, what business is Harley Davidson in? We could answer motorcycles and be right from the company perspective but no one would spend the amount of money they do to buy just a motorcycle. Their competitors make equal or better products at significantly lower prices. The customer is buying a Harley–complete with the image of being a rebel, an outlaw, freedom, an American institution, a rugged individualist, etc. The success of Harley Davidson depends on continuing to develop, maintain and serve that image. That is their business from the customer's point of view.

One of the things I have discovered in the consulting business is that I never know who my next customer will be, who will refer them to me or why they will buy my services. I do know that if I continue to write, speak, teach and tell people what I do and do it well, then I will continue to attract clients. Having asked many clients why they hire me, I can generally define my clients as high growth or struggling businesses that are interested in designing and implementing change. I am thus in the business of designing and implementing change and my customers are high growth or struggling businesses. I used to think I was a management consultant. What business are you in? ■

Discussion Questions:

1. What business are you in? How could you redefine your business from your customers' perspective?

2. What is your competitive edge? What makes you unique?

Outrageous Managers create community with their customers.

Marketing 101

A retail company creates expensive brochures, materials and sales tools to market their products but never defines or targets their customers. They go out of business.

A restaurant company creatively and effectively markets only a few new properties and loses sales in the majority of their restaurants. Overall sales are down.

An industrial supplier loses track of their product costs and only sells products that lose them money. They go under.

A pulp and paper company creates private labels for all their customers—large and small. They lose money and create huge warehousing and distribution problems.

Most of us erroneously equate marketing with advertising and the media. When we do that, we fall victim to the myth that marketing is very complicated, sophisticated and beyond our capabilities. Actually, marketing is a very simple and straightforward process for most companies and can be done by anyone who learns the basics and follows through. The major mistakes made in the marketing arena are usually those that violate the basics, or what I call Marketing 101. Advertising and the media are alternative ways of implementing a carefully designed marketing plan but never replace that plan.

So, back to basics. What are the key elements of a marketing plan and program?

1. Make marketing a philosophy practiced by everyone in the business. We can only survive, prosper and profit by identifying and satisfying the needs of the customer.

2. Analyze the marketplace. How big is it? Can it support the business?

   Who is the customer? What do they need? Why will they buy from us?

   Who are the key competitors? What is our share? What is our niche?

   What is the environment? How does it affect us and our customers?

3. Define the marketing mix–the four "P"s

   Product. What are our products or services? Relate each product or service to specific customer needs

   Price. How will we price our products to best serve our customers? Are we the best product or the lowest price? Competitive?

   Place. Where does our customer need each product or service? What is the best way to deliver? Can they find us? Great service?

   Promotion. What is the best way to reach our customers? What advertising, selling or other programs best reach the customer? How do we develop working relationships with our customers? Who will develop and maintain those relationships?

4. Plan and manage the marketing programs–continually review the marketplace, industry trends, competitor programs, the four "P"s and your sales data. Talk to your customers and ask how you can serve them better. Ensure that everyone

in your business is customer oriented and dedicated to serving your customers.

Master the basics of marketing through developing and maintaining excellent working relationships with your customers. ■

Discussion Questions:

1. Are your marketing programs complicated and hard to understand? How?

2 Is everyone involved in your marketing programs?

Outrageous Managers master the basics of marketing.

Market Research

*A*major industrial supplier set up a new company to manufacture and distribute what they expected to be a hot new product. The product did not meet safety standards and the company failed before it ever got going–at a very high cost.

A major builder of environmental equipment for the electric utility industry set up a national marketing and sales staff to call on potential customers. They only had about five potential customers per year so they wasted their marketing dollars and failed to focus on the real customers. They also frustrated their sales force, diminishing their effectiveness.

Market research is easy and almost all businesses do some research to define their customers and their needs. Unfortunately, most companies also make some basic mistakes that can seriously affect their business results. The most common mistakes are:

- Assuming that they know who the customer is and what they want.

- Asking the wrong questions or focusing on the wrong issue.

- Allowing their own views or preferences to substitute for customer wants and needs.

- Complicating the process and making it mysterious or difficult.

- Creating laborious surveys or instruments to collect useless data.

- Emphasizing the volume of data collected rather than the quality of inputs.

- Not believing the information received if it doesn't match their vision.

- Not following through and using the market research to define marketing plans.

Market research is a continuous process of gathering information and feedback from customers, suppliers, competitors, industry analysts, employees, the community worked in and many secondary sources. It is the life blood and information flow of marketing efforts. The most important aspects of market research are to:

1. Design it to support business plans.

2 Use the easily available sources to gather the information. Don't complicate it.

3. Summarize and analyze the information to make it usable.

4. Actually believe and use the information to define effective marketing approaches.

There are many free and easy sources for market research data and inputs. The best sources are always direct contacts with customers, competitors and suppliers. It never ceases to amaze me how much people will tell you about their work and companies if they are asked. So, ask! Then compile statistical and background data on the industry, community or business through secondary sources. The Internet is fast becoming a great data source and the old sources still work, including libraries, government publications, research reports, trade associations, investment analysts, annual reports, magazines and journals and countless other sources.

Market research works when we keep it simple and then use the data to manage our marketing programs. Remember to get direct information when possible. Talking to our customers and competitors can be fun and very profitable. ∎

Discussion Questions:

1. Do you really know what your customers want and need? Prove it!

2. What information are you ignoring or burying about your business? Why?

Outrageous Mangers use market research to define marketing programs.

Benchmarking—
Is Your Company
Competitive?

*A*n attorney was concerned with profitability. He believed revenues were above average for his size firm, but felt profits were lower than average. A trip to the law library and a review of the current law office management magazines showed he was well above average on revenue but staffing and costs were way out of line.

A floor covering business wanted to confirm data about key sales, operational and financial statistics before proceeding with the due diligence phase of an acquisition. For $75 they purchased their association's current comparative business report. It proved invaluable in measuring the value and performance of the potential acquisition.

Benchmarking is a key planning, marketing and performance tool. For a minimal investment of time and expense, extensive information is available that can help you measure how well you are doing compared to similar businesses and your competitors. Many businesses have done very well in boom markets. But when the environment changed, they failed because they were not really competitive and had no clear advantage in serving their customers. All businesses go through cycles. Businesses that are prepared for all the different cycles, maintain a competitive edge and adapt to the changing conditions will survive and prosper.

Benchmarking is a simple way to keep track of how we are doing and to define areas that need attention. Knowing our industry and the operating environment helps prepare us for upcoming challenges and opportunities. The process is straightforward. Sources for competitive information are readily available. To benchmark your business:

- Join your trade, industry and professional associations or read their publications.

- Check government sources for demographics, general industry statistics and guidelines.

- Read competitors' annual reports for very useful market and financial data.

- Talk to vendors, suppliers, bankers, attorneys, accountants and consultants.

- Use the library for key industry financial ratios and other published sources.

- Have your local librarian search for information for you.

- Connect with your local university and have them do studies for you.

- Surf the Internet for industry data, starting at any of the major search engines.

- Go to national or regional conventions and talk to others in your industry.

The keys are to keep it simple and get the information you need to compare your business performance and data to the results of your competitors. Look for areas that need improvement and attention. Also look for opportunities and growth areas. Find your competitive edge. ■

Discussion Questions:

1. How do you compare to your competitors? How do you know?

2. What is your competitive edge? Will it carry you through the down cycles?

Outrageous Managers develop a competitive edge.

Due Diligence

A large company acquired another large company and put some of their existing divisions under the management of one of their new divisions. *The new manager was technically weak and made major product mistakes that cost several hundred million dollars.*

Two companies merged to gain apparent market synergy and improved market positioning. They were unable to work together and the gains were never realized.

A manufacturing company appeared to be an excellent buy to expand the capabilities and market position of another manufacturer. During the due diligence process, it was discovered that they had exaggerated their profits by consistently deferring needed maintenance and capital improvements. The acquisition was canceled.

Due diligence is the process of examining the true viability and risk associated with potential mergers, acquisitions or new ventures. It is usually done within 30 days and is a comprehensive review of the existing condition and future potential of the company or business to be entered. In transactions by public companies, it is normally a required step in the process. It is recommended as a step for all businesses entering new areas. The process always includes a detailed financial review of the transaction. It also normally includes a look at the marketing of the business and a look at the management and administration to define potential cost savings. These are all necessary and positive steps but don't go far enough. The condensed time and urgency of completing a deal usually hurry the process to the point that mistakes are made, the process is not broad enough, or the findings are not implemented.

Some suggestions for improving the process and helping to define acquisitions, mergers or new ventures that will succeed are outlined below:

- Include both companies or businesses in the process. Try for a win-win outcome.

- Have an objective outsider lead the process (not involved in the deal or the outcome).

- Make the process broad enough to define all the potential benefits and risks.

- Ensure that the positive parts of the new venture or combination are a significant part of the process—look for the potential synergy and benefits.

- Concentrate on substance and data as well as intuition and opinion.

- Visit and observe all facilities and operations. Talk to the managers and workers.

- Benchmark the business versus other businesses in the marketplace.

- Bring both businesses together to visualize how the new integration will work.

- Document all the findings and ensure that they are converted into a detailed plan for implementing the new entity.

During the due diligence process, it is important to pay special attention to business and technical risks and the current business and technical environment. This analysis can include reviews of the: backlog; budgets; capital requirements; contractual exposures;

operating strengths and weaknesses; market positioning; technical capability; management capability; project performance; performance measures; quality of
products and services; policies and procedures;
turnover of key people; labor situation; organization
and approach to doing business; level of automation;
maintenance and condition of facilities.

The due diligence process can be extensive and
sometimes expensive. Make sure you get the benefits
by truly understanding all the ramifications of the
proposed actions and how to realize the benefits. The
most common mistake is to believe that the integration will be easy after the deal is completed. Actually
getting the proposed benefits takes a lot of planning,
leadership and perseverance. The due diligence
process can start the planning and the due diligence
team can play a significant role in helping to lead the
integration.

Get all the benefits you can from the due diligence process. Due diligence can be an important
strategic planning tool even if the deal falls through. ■

Discussion Questions:

1. Forget the deal for a minute (This is hard), what
   will you really gain from the proposed action?
   What are the costs? What are the benefits? Can
   the benefits truly be realized?

2. How will you implement the proposed action?
   Who will lead the implementation and what
   resources will they need? Are there clear goals
   and time lines? Can you do it?

**Outrageous Managers exercise due diligence on
major decisions.**

The Business
Role of Process

A *major state agency concentrates on 'teams' and
emphasizes personal process. Great resistance is
encountered and they experience a major strike.
Performance declines.*

*A board of directors concentrates on how they relate to each
other and loses sight of the business. They communicate well but
avoid the tough business issues. No progress.*

Many businesses today are concerned about
good process and this is very healthy. Process is
about *how* we communicate, lead, meet, coach and
deal with conflict. Process defines how we involve
others in our plans and projects, make decisions, create, and solve problems. Major programs in large and
small businesses however have been launched to
improve process independent of business goals and
objectives. These are usually very expensive and not
very effective. The goal of good process is to energize
the workplace, to improve planning and performance
and to achieve business goals. Process is the method
used, not the goal. Concentrating on process by itself
can be as dangerous as having poor process.

The key to developing good process is to do it in
the context of doing business. Leaders and professional business people are excited about their business
and want to make it succeed. Learning process in this
context builds on the excitement, aims for immediate

and tangible results and works from a place of safety and comfort.

The pure process approach has us concentrate on individual failings and personal issues. How many of us really want to spend a lot of time at work dealing with our personal issues, being confronted by others, or having our fears and insecurities made public? No one I know enjoys those sessions or changes their behavior at work because of them.

Some key insights I have learned about developing good process are:

- Select the appropriate process to accomplish the specific business goals.

- Measure the success by measuring specific performance improvement and results.

- Process models will not overcome management and commitment issues.

- Committed managers and leaders will personalize and adapt process models.

- Limited duration task teams with specific goals work very well.

- Individuals resist changes that go against group norms; so process changes with groups.

- Individuals and groups must be intrinsically motivated to change.

- Interpersonal process helps individual growth but not work group performance.

- Avoid top down approaches where the top dictates but does not participate or change.

- Survey and feedback methods take too long and are not effective.

- Integrate process into what you do and into your leaders and projects.

- Train existing managers to be process oriented in their daily activities.

Process is a critical part of business success. Integrating good process into our businesses will increase performance, promote creativity and make work a lot more fun. ■

Discussion Questions:

1. Are your teams and processes tied to specific business goals and deadlines? Have you let process get in the way of measuring and demanding performance?

2. Do your processes serve your business well? Have you gone too far? Have you gone far enough? Do your managers use effective process in their day to day work?

Outrageous Managers align their processes with their business goals.

Creative Hiring

*T*he key to success used to be a creative strategy or creative marketing approaches. Many companies know how to do that today but can't find the people they need to design and implement the strategies and plans. It is now time to apply our creative energy to recruiting and retaining the best people. The old solutions of placing an ad or hiring a recruiting firm will no longer produce the desired outcomes.

Actually, in the technology area and many related fields, it is downright scary to try to get and keep the people you want. You have to get creative and try new ways. You also need to give this area the resources, priority and attention it needs if you are going to succeed. Here are some examples of creative hiring methods that have succeeded:

- Using creative recruiting teams from all parts of the company.

- Putting your best marketing people on the recruiting teams and using their expertise.

- Defining the type of people you really want–not just job descriptions.

- Conducting focus groups with the type of people you want–usually with people who work for your competitors.

- Going to festivals, fairs, programs and venues where the people you want hang out.

- Simplifying the hiring process to get to good decisions quickly.

- Using your employees as recruiters to bring in friends and acquaintances.

- Matching candidates with mentors to help them feel comfortable with the company and process.

- Acquiring competitors to get their people.

Once you hire people and get them on board, you are not done. The same process that allowed you to lure people from your competitors will be applied to you if you don't continue the creativity and apply it to retaining your people. This will take even more attention, priority and resources than the recruiting program. Some creative approaches that have worked include:

- Keep the work interesting and challenging.

- Have creativity days and encourage new ideas and approaches.

- Don't assign retention responsibility to HR. Make it a line responsibility.

- Allow people to find where they belong in the organization. Don't box them in.

- Keep organizations open and fluid.

- Encourage and support learning new skills and abilities.

- Celebrate and reward accomplishments–often and generously.

- Pay people what they are worth.

- Include the families in rewards and celebrations.

These are just a few suggestions. To really be successful in recruiting and retaining the best people, you will need to create many new ways to make it work. Go for it! ■

Discussion Questions:

1. Who are the creative leaders in your organization? Are they involved in hiring and retaining your key people?

2. What two new ways can you use to hire new people? What two new ways can you use to retain your key people?

Outrageous Managers are wildly creative recruiters.

Getting The People You Want

In addition to being wildly creative, companies need solid hiring processes to get and retain the people they want. The benefits of using solid hiring practices include:

- The ability to make better hiring decisions.

- Less time and effort spent to prepare for interviews.

- Less time spent interviewing and increased interviewing effectiveness.

- More confidence in the hiring process.

- Better assimilation of new hires into your company.

- Clearly establishing the knowledge, skills and abilities of the candidates, as well as their fit into their new position, new team and new company.

- Better knowledge of your company by the candidates.

The Hiring Process

The key elements of a successful hiring process include:

- Creating a recruiting plan. The recruiting plan will define the overall process.

- Defining the level and compensation for the new position.

- Creating and using flexible job descriptions and lists of key attributes.

- Defining and scheduling a recruiting team that will normally consist of the hiring manager, a functional manager, an experienced peer in the same function, a team member of the new hire and perhaps a corporate officer or the president for key hires.

- Defining the process to be used for recruiting potential candidates and assigning responsibilities for advertising, recruiting, hiring search firms, networking, screening resumes, selecting candidates for interviews, reference checking, etc.

- Defining the interview process and assigning responsibilities, including conducting technical interviews, in depth background coverage, probing behavioral questions and an in-depth probing behavioral interview.

- Defining the decision making process–how will the entire recruiting team meet to reach a consensus decision. Who will make the final decision?

- Extending the offer and closing the candidate– the offer should be extended within 24 hours of the decision and followed up the same day with a formal written offer. The responsible manager should close the candidate and upon acceptance ensure that the new hire receives a congratulatory letter and an appropriate gift (such as flowers or a food basket) at their home within 48 hours of acceptance.

• Defining and assigning responsibilities for personally managing the indoctrination and assimilation of the new hires.

The keys to the hiring process are to ensure that people are excited about being part of the process and that the responsibilities, decisions and actions are clear. The process also needs to be quick and decisive. Any process that goes on for more than two weeks is excessive, will lose key recruits and costs too much. ∎

Discussion Questions:

1. How long does your hiring process take? How can you shorten it?

2. Do you trust your process? Your intuition? Your recruiting teams?

Outrageous Managers hire quickly and wisely.

Performance Measurement

A *large government agency initiates a comprehensive per-*
formance program with computerized measures and
multiple variables. The managers and employees turn
it into a game and play the system instead of improving perfor-
mance.

A large chemical manufacturer sets up hard to reach goals
and manages promotions and rewards based on reaching the
targets. The managers manipulate inventory and quality to
ensure their goals are reached. Every time a manager moves, mil-
lions of dollars of inventory are written off.

A recruiting firm sets up a performance measurement sys-
tem with eight to ten variables and the recruiters don't pay atten-
tion to any of them.

A high technology firm sets one or two easily measured
goals for each manager every year and their performance soars.

Performance measurement is a crucial part of
any performance improvement program. It is also the
part that seems to take the longest to design and
implement and the part that keeps the program from
becoming successful. The KISS theory is the most
important part of any successful measurement program–keep it simple! A few principles may help:

- Measure the end result you want to accomplish.
  Not the steps along the way.

- Be specific and quantitative. Qualitative measures don't work.

- If you can't quantify it. Don't measure it.

- Measure what you can easily measure with your accounting, budgeting or operating system. Don't create a new system.

- Limit the number of measures at any time to four or less. Less is better and the more you measure, the less attention is paid to each measure.

- Keep one or two of the measures the same over time. These should be the one or two key end results that ensure business results and success.

- Change one or two measures each quarter to deal with specific performance problems or to introduce new approaches and procedures.

- Make sure **everyone** is held accountable and receives reports on their performance at least weekly. Receiving feedback on performance is critical to improvement.

- Take action when people fail to meet goals. Deal with it immediately and clearly.

- Performance plans should be defined for all people not meeting their goals and then the plans must be enforced. Allowing people to not meet goals kills performance.

- Take action when people exceed goals. Reward them quickly and often.

- Almost meeting goals is not acceptable.

Performance measurement is very important and should be very easy. A simple, well managed system will work well and deliver the desired business results. ■

Discussion Questions:

1. Is your performance measurement system simple and clear? Is it easy to use?

2. Does your system work? Are you achieving the results you want? Why not?

Outrageous Managers measure performance and get results.

Accountability– The Key To Performance

Accountability is the process that completes the business planning and performance loop. It ties your planning, budgeting, financial and operational reporting processes to your performance system. Accountability is the link that ensures that follow-through happens and results are achieved. Many companies have business plans and budgets, and measure their progress and performance in great detail. These functions set direction, responsibility, and measure results. Accountability without these is impossible and yet planning does not guarantee accountability. Accountability is the personal and dynamic process where expectations and results are discussed and exceptions are explored and dealt with.

Accountability is a personal quality that must be developed and demanded of all people in your business, including yourself. Performance suffers when either of two common practices occur. The first is not holding employees accountable, the second is not having someone to hold us accountable. Employee accountability requires constant attention and follow-up. Let your employees know what you expect, let them perform their job, and then follow up. Follow-up requires regular meetings to review how things are going and the important performance factors. Keep those meetings factual and data based. At the end of each meeting, make a list of action items with due dates and be sure each one is reviewed at a future meeting. Start your next meeting by reviewing the action items from the last meeting. Failure to complete action items on time must have consequences–without action at this point, there is no accountability.

Managers and business owners struggle with their own accountability. Who is going to hold you accountable for achieving what you said you wanted to achieve? Accountability is not just for others, we must model accountability and hold ourselves accountable as well. We need someone to review with us what is working and what is not working within our company, and why. We also need someone to hold us accountable for doing what we said we would do. This review should be done with someone you trust and whose opinion you value. Your management team, peers, mentor, attorney, accountant, business consultant or another business owner may be able to serve in this capacity. Provide them with your business plan and budget. Agree to review your business and financial results with them monthly or at least quarterly. Preparing for this meeting is an important step toward achieving and modeling accountability.

Accountability is not an optional business process. The routine measurement of progress throughout the year keeps you and your business on track. Create an accountability process for you and your business today! Big surprises are rare when accountability is practiced routinely. Surprises are the norm when accountability is absent. Accountability happens when action, commitment and follow-through come together. The key is to keep track of assigned actions, follow up and ensure they have taken place and take action when deadlines are missed. ■

Discussion Questions:

1. Does your business operate on accountability or excuses?

2. Who holds you accountable?

Outrageous Managers demand total accountability.

Management Accounting

A *new restaurant created a wonderful environment in a great location. Their fixed costs were too high and they could never show a profit.*

A manufacturing company developed their manufacturing processes based on inaccurate product flows. They lost money on each unit sold and went under.

Most new restaurants and new businesses fail. There are many reasons, but a recurring theme is that the owners or managers didn't understand the basics of accounting and finance. Managers don't need to become accountants or get an MBA. Managers do need to understand the basics and know how to make decisions based on financial and accounting information and reports. This is the general field of management accounting.

There are two major accounting reports and processes managers need to master–the income statement and the budget. There are also two financial reports and processes that managers need to master–the balance sheet and the statement of sources and uses of funds or cash flow. Each of these four reports contains information that is critical to understanding the present and projected financial condition of your business.

The income statement, or profit and loss statement, reports actual revenues and expenses and shows whether or not you are making a profit. The revenues or sales are the dollars of income that have been booked during the period of time that the report covers. Income statements are always tied to a period of time–a month, a quarter or a year. The revenues are the scorecard of the marketing and sales group in your company. Only actual, documented sales get reported in the income statement so this report separates the fiction of projections and guesses from the clear facts of actual results.

The expense or cost portion of the income statement shows the corresponding costs for the same period as the revenues. All the costs that have actually been spent are reported. The expenses or costs are the report card of your operating and management group. The costs include direct and indirect costs, fixed and variable costs, labor and materials, overhead costs, and sales, general and administrative costs. Understanding the different types of costs and how they affect your business can be critical. Managing these costs is essential.

The major management tool that is used to manage the revenues and costs is the budget. The budget projects each revenue stream and its related costs and then reports the actual revenues and costs vs the projected revenues and costs. The budget measures and reports whether we did what we said we would do. Budgets are internal reports for us to manage the business. The role of accounting is to collect, verify and report the data. The role of management is to define the information that is needed and then use the reports to manage the business and make decisions based on the information. Budgets frequently get too cumbersome and are used only by the accountants because management doesn't understand the budgets or defers to accounting to select what is important. Budgets need to remain simple and to be management tools–not accounting tools.

The balance sheet is a financial snapshot at a given date. The balance sheet is the scorecard of the finance and administration group within your business. It covers the financial issues such as cash, inventory, receivables and payables. It also reports the treasury issues of assets, liabilities and owners or shareholders equity. The balance sheet is the money management report. The income statement is normally based on accrual accounting which means that we report it as it is booked, not paid for. The balance sheet is about the actual flow of money. Income and cash are very different. High growth companies normally make a lot of income but require major infusions of cash to stay liquid. Understanding cash flows is as important as revenues and expenses. The sources and uses of funds statement shows the actual cash flows for a period of time. It is a more complex report but necessary to understand the business.

The financing of the company is the subject of the balance sheet. Investment that owners or shareholders put into the company as well as loans and other debt are recorded, as well as the use of that money in buildings, equipment or working capital. The equity portion of the balance sheet is the owners scorecard. It reports on the value of the investment.

Financial and accounting reports are very valuable management tools when we understand them and manage them. Many investment firms, banks and agencies such as the SBA put on free or low cost seminars and programs on the basics of understanding accounting and finance. Make sure you understand them and use them to manage your business. ■

Discussion Questions:

1. Do you really understand balance sheets, income statements and budgets? Do you really understand your financial condition?

2. How can you improve your financial performance? Who will help you?

Outrageous Managers continually improve their financial condition.

Business Models

Would you buy a $75,000 Mercedes Benz without taking it for a spin around the block? How about a $20,000 Chevrolet? A $300 mountain bicycle? Would you buy a $100 dress or a $40 shirt without trying them on for size? I didn't think so!

But have you ever adjusted the prices of your products or services on a whim? Committed to a sales commission structure without really knowing how much the payoff could cost your business? Or decided on a direct mail campaign without calculating how much you will have to sell in order to break-even?

Most of us have processes for making decisions that allow us to quickly size up a situation and decide whether or not we are going to invest our money on a particular person, place or thing. These processes range from snap judgments to extensive and pro-tracted analysis. At times we get stuck because today's business decisions are often complex and the outcomes uncertain. So is there an alternative between guessing and analysis paralysis?

Yes! First get clear on what's important to your business. When you're clear on your objectives, decisions become simpler. If you're not clear, it's amazing how much time and money you can waste looking at opportunities that are clearly out of your expertise or beyond the scope of your business. Use your business plan to stay clear on your objectives.

Then develop a business model based on your plan and your financial and operating information. These models can use simple spreadsheets or more detailed and complex simulation packages. The model should be able to tell you the gross impact of decisions on your key operating and financial measures. Don't get too fancy with the modeling, use factors that have significant impacts on the business. Also use available software to do the work for you. If modeling isn't your specialty, get someone to help you but don't make it a big or expensive project.

An integrated model allows you to forecast the impact of any business decision you are considering. Models that are particularly helpful to young businesses allow them to price new products, evaluate sales and marketing plans and project cash flows. The key to these models is identifying the elements that drive your business and having these as separate cells in your spreadsheet or simulation so that you can play what-if games.

The benefit of creating a what-if model is having the capability to input different unit forecasts, prices, discounts, promotions, product costs and other variables and see the results immediately. The impact of testing a decision under multiple scenarios is very valuable. Also, the risk is a lot less than trying the same decision on your top ten products, customers, or employees.

Keep your business model simple. Use historical data and percents as reference points. Build your model around the 80/20 rule. It does not have to be perfect for it to have value or give you the confidence to move forward.

Remember, models are only useful if you understand them and use them. All key managers should understand the business model and use it in making key decisions. ■

Discussion Questions:

1. How do you make key business and financial decisions? Do they get the results you want? How do you know?

2. Can you create a simple model of your business? Who could help you? When will it be in place?

Outrageous Managers use simple business decision models.

Business Processes

A manufacturer designs and implements major new systems to increase productivity. They automate the existing ways of doing business and fail to achieve the benefits.

A retailer implements new point of sale and financial systems to improve operations but fails to look at their business processes. They automate outdated approaches.

Designing and implementing new systems doesn't necessarily solve our business problems, it frequently just performs the old ways of doing business faster. New technologies and systems can improve our businesses if we also look at how technology changes our business and changes how we do business–in other words our business processes.

Business processes are the integrated system of policies, procedures, approaches, common practices and specific steps that we use to conduct business. They may be formal and written, or more generally, informal and learned through on the job training and work experience. Business processes are the ways we have learned to get the job done. Over time, the business practices become comfortable and routine–even when they make little or no sense. Archaic business practices are not limited to manufacturing or operations–they creep into the ways we do finance, accounting, marketing, selling, technical projects, human resources, training, communication, management, performance measurement and all areas of the business. They become ingrained and almost invisible as they become accepted practice. They can also be expensive and business threatening.

An excellent time to look at our business processes and see if they still serve us is when we are considering new technologies or systems. Designing and implementing new systems requires extensive change anyway, so we might as well change our business processes as we change our systems. The other reason for doing both changes simultaneously is to ensure that we don't automate outdated or inefficient processes.

So, how do we go about reviewing and redefining our business processes?

1. Create safety–the goal is to improve the process, not fire people.

2. Form a task force of internal and external investigators–the internal members know the business but may be attached to the present methods and the external members will have excellent observation skills and objectivity, but don't know your business.

3. Document the existing business processes and systems in detail and in writing.

4. Use the task force and management to brainstorm alternatives and desired outcomes.

5. Work interactively and collaboratively with the system designers to analyze alternatives and define those that are feasible and provide the best return.

6. Define and implement a change management program to review proposed changes with those who will be involved. Modify proposals to

determine the best implementable solutions that the managers and workers will support. Include training and/or processing of the changes in the program.

7. Follow through and ensure the changes are implemented and work.

One of the key aspects of managing the changes in business processes is to set very aggressive time lines for analysis and completion and then stick to them. Any process that takes longer than two months loses momentum and doesn't get implemented. ■

Discussion Questions:

1. Are your business processes competitive and supporting your plan? How do you know?

2. What management systems are you using? Are they producing the results you want? How would you change them? When?

Outrageous Managers insist on excellent business processes.

Celebrating Victories

Yahoo! Whoopee! Eureka! Yeah! All right! Way to go! Good job! These are all ways to celebrate some business accomplishment or victory. They are a good start but true celebrations need to go further. We have made plans, set goals, measured performance and done very well. Now we have to finish the process by celebrating the results. This is not hard, it's fun. It's also crucial.

A lot of people downplay receiving awards and recognition for their work. That is fine. But if they don't get the awards, the rewards and the recognition, watch out! We work so hard to achieve our victories, so let's not lose the impact by forgetting to award and reward. This step seals the present victory and ensures that there will be more to come.

What is the best way to celebrate? A combination of awards and rewards is called for. Awards are the symbolic gifts that are significant within the company and provide recognition for the achievement. Rewards are the significant monetary or related compensation that share the benefits that the company experienced because of the achievement. Some guidelines for celebrations include:

- Celebrate and reward frequently–weekly is great–monthly is minimal.

- Put a lot of thought and energy into what to reward and how to reward the recipients.

- Make a big deal about the awards and rewards.
- Have the key executives involved or the CEO make the awards.
- Keep it fresh by changing the responsible people.
- Consistency is important but so is spontaneity and creativity.
- Don't let ceremonies get habitual and stale where they lose their impact.
- We are all different and like to be rewarded in unique ways based on who we are.
- Awards can be similar for differing accomplishments.
- Team awards can be fun and meaningful.
- Rewards are personal.
- Rewards need to be commensurate with the magnitude and impact of the accomplishment.
- Rewards need to be tangible and significant.
- Including entertainment or music can help set the festive tone that is desired.
- Never award or reward behavior that is less than acceptable performance or just meets minimum standards.

Celebration in the form of awards and rewards is a key part of any performance measurement and performance improvement program. The awards and rewards should directly tie to the measures and should only be given for results. When people exceed performance and deliver exceptional results, we should be happy to reward them and share the profits and benefits that those results have produced. Awards are fun ways to recognize that excellent performance.

Rewards are the raises, gifts, dollars or other tangible ways of sharing the wealth and assuring the future excellence. ■

Discussion Questions:

1. How do you celebrate your accomplishments and victories?

2. How do you reward and celebrate outstanding performance?

Outrageous Managers celebrate and reward outstanding performance.

Chapter 2
Leading
Change

Change is a journey. It has a starting point and a direction but we never really know where it will take us. Whether talking about changing our groups, our organizations, or ourselves, the process of change takes us down many pathways and leads us to new places, both internally and externally. The simplest changes can lead to totally unexpected results, some of which can even be viewed as positive.

Change is a choice. No individual, group or organization can be forced to change. We can pretend to change when others demand that we act in different ways but apparent compliance does not mean that any real change has taken place. If we make a conscious decision that we want to change, then the start of the change process will begin. Choice is the start of the journey. We can also choose not to change and that is also the start of a journey.

Change is personal. Whether we are changing technology, business processes or organizations, the changes will be personally felt and processed by everyone involved and affected. Relationships will change and each person affected will make decisions based on their personal perceptions and experiences. Since personal reactions and consequences are not predictable, change follows its own course. The human elements of change are the key elements of designing and implementing change.

Change is interactive and interpersonal. It rarely happens in isolation. We usually change when interactions with others invite and encourage us to change. When we change, it changes our relationships with others and starts to change the groups and systems where we work and live. Small personal changes can have far reaching and global impacts. Our relationships are the basic building blocks of change and the change process.

Each change project changes the change agent as well as the managers, workers, groups, and organizations affected by the change. No one can embark on a journey of change without being open to change themselves. If you do not want to change, do not start a change journey–it won't go anywhere.

This chapter is about the journey of change. It includes some theory, a lot of practical suggestions, and a framework for trying to understand the journey. Embarking on the journey of change takes a lot of courage. This module is about learning to navigate the journey of change and to steer a successful course. The goal is to understand the journey and to be able to make informed decisions that can start the journey in the right direction and provide the information to make the frequent course corrections that will be required. Controlling change is an illusion–it can't be done.

Leading change can be done if we are willing to create shared visions of the desired future state, embrace the journey and keep a clear eye on the goals we are trying to reach. It is not easy. Successful change requires leadership, knowledge, courage, innovation, openness, skill, and a lot of energy.

Change Models

The paths to successful change are defined by the type of change that is happening or needs to happen and the depth of the change required. Organizations don't change unless the groups that comprise that organization change; and groups don't change unless the individuals that comprise that group change. It is not necessary for all the groups or all the individuals to change; a critical mass of groups and individuals must change to achieve successful organization change. The paths of individual change, group change and organization change are different paths.

The other major factor that determines the paths of successful change are the depths of change required. Conscious changes or outer changes in behavior and actions are the easiest type of change and are defined here as first level changes. Second level changes, such as system changes, function changes and career changes, are more inner directed and involve the subconscious factors that drive the outer actions and behaviors. Second level changes are similar to double loop learning in that they change not only the outer action but the programming that has determined how those actions take place. Third level changes such as life changes, purpose changes or culture changes, go another level deeper and require changes in the unconscious forces that shape the meaning of the first and second order factors.

The combination of the three types of change with the three levels of change results in a matrix that defines the nine paths of change. The Nine Paths of Change that form the basis for this module are outlined in the following matrix and then described below. The model depicts how the paths of change interact and how the process of change becomes more complex as the paths go deeper.

The Nine Paths of Organization Change

	Individual	Group	Organization
Change	**Behavior Change**	**Rule Change**	**Procedure Change**
Ego, single loop One Dimensional Attitude, Action, Rules Body, Outer Driven	Attitude, Action Performance	Norms, Procedures Objectives	Practices, Preferences Plans, Objecties
Management	*Corrective Action*	*Team Training*	*Training*
Transition	**Career Change**	**Role Change**	**System Change**
Superego, Double loop Two Dimensional Values, Mind, Emotion Roles, Subconscious	Roles, Values Personal Goals	Process, Values Goals	Policy, Principles Strategy, Mission
Leadership	*Coaching*	*Team Development*	*Org. Learning*
Transformation	**Life Change**	**Purpose Change**	**Transfor-mation**
Id., Triple loop Three Dimensional Beliefs, Archetypes Soul, Unconscious	Beliefs, Drives Life Purpose	Beliefs, Unifying Force Overarching Vision Purpose	Symbols, Mythology Collective Unconscious
Transpersonal Leadership	*Mentoring*	*Team Transformation*	*Organization Transformation*

Levels of the Nine Paths of Change

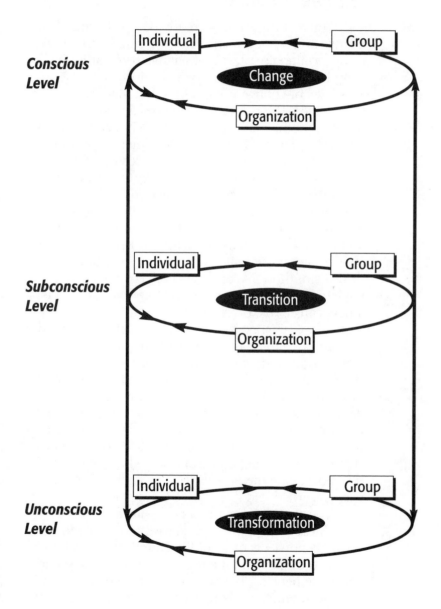

Each path is discussed and explored below.

"Simple" Change

The first three paths are the paths of "simple" change and management. They are simple only in reference to the other levels of change. They are still complicated and take energy and effort to do well. This level of change works at the rational or conscious level. The changes can be designed or engineered and the main objective is to change actions or behaviors. The new desired state is defined and then a path is developed to lead from the existing state to the new desired state. The paths are rational or mental paths that look at very specific actions or behaviors that are on the surface and easily understood. People may not like the change but they can understand it and learn the new ways of acting or behaving. These changes are those that stay within the existing abilities or fields of those making the change. They do not have to learn whole new areas of knowledge or adapt a new career, role or system.

Simple change is as close as we get to managed change. Something is done a certain way now and we want it done a different way. The processes are straightforward and the results are implemented and measured. The first keys to simple change are to describe the change in detail, be very clear about the new desired state, and then train the individual, group or organization on how to do the new action or procedure. The training is action oriented and concentrates on doing the new procedure so that the new way is learned and the change takes place.

The second keys are to deal with the change itself. Most of us don't change easily. We need to have some acknowledgement of the change process, the ability to understand the reasons for the change and know the benefits that are anticipated. Buying in and understanding the rationale are necessary even at this level of change. The difference at this level from the other levels is that choice is not present. The changes are top down and will be implemented. An organization decision has already taken place and we immediately go to the implementation process. The acknowledgement of the process and the rationale are built into the training process that implements the change.

This type of change also includes behavior changes that are needed without new designs. This occurs when individuals or groups are not performing at the desired level and are not following established procedures. Management corrective action defines the performance issue and the desired state and then defines the process to get from the existing state to the desired state. This can involve retraining or increased supervision.

Transition

The second level of change increases in complexity and difficulty from the first level. Transitions involve changes in careers, skills, roles, values, and systems. These changes go beyond the rational mind and involve the subconscious as well as the conscious mind. They involve double loop learning. Double loop learning means that we look not only at the action or behavior but at the internal controls or programs that cause that behavior. The simplest explanation of double loop learning is to picture a thermostat for your heating system. Changing the thermostat to adjust the temperature is a single loop action. Changing the heating system or reprogramming the thermostat to adjust to changing desires of whether we are hot or cold is a double loop action. We look not only at the temperature but our desires about what is comfortable and alternatives about how to achieve that.

Behavioral models normally suggest that our actions are determined by our internal beliefs, attitudes or values and the situations we encounter. The first level of change looked only at the outer action. This level of change involves looking at the attitudes and values that drive the outer action, the double loop. Transitions always involve changes in some of those attitudes and values. Since our attitudes and values reside in our subconscious, we cannot successfully transition without processes that explore the subconscious and change some of the variables that are driving our outer behavior. In other words, we need to process and reframe our actions and our behaviors and change the systems that drive those behaviors.

The subconscious or what Freud called the superego is the controller of a collection of feelings and values about how we should act in the world. This area of our psyche is where we store all the messages we have taken in about how to be and act. It has been described as the repository of all the parental and authoritative messages learned as a child and while in school. It is the conscience that lets us know when we are doing something we shouldn't do.

Transitions thus involve processes to explore what has been driving our behavior and to look at replacing some of the old values or attitudes with new ones that will lead to new actions and behaviors. For example, a woman carried in her subconscious the maxim from her father that women should never make over $20,000 per year. She continually stalled out at that level until she explored the reasons for not moving ahead. Once she was aware that her father's maxim was determining her behavior, she could change it and move forward. She then became highly successful without limitations.

The process keys are to explore the reasons for the old behaviors, determine the values or attitudes that have been shaping them and then change them to support the new actions or behaviors. These processes involve dealing with the mental systems and emotional systems that determine our behavior. Both the mental pictures or models that determine our thought patterns and the emotional feelings that spur our actions must be processed and changed to successfully transition. These processes take time, leadership and commitment. We cannot simply demand transitions or manage them in a top down way. Those involved must be included in the process and led through the change processes.

Transition always involves choice. Some people may choose to make the transitions necessary and others will choose not to. The motivation to make the transitions must become internal in the individuals and groups and they must make an active decision for the transition to be accomplished. Thus the reasons for the transition must be compelling and very well explained and examined. The individuals and groups can then be invited to make the transitions and many of them will undergo the process. Success, however, is never assured. The reasons for the transition may be compelling to the organization but not to the individual. The individual reasons for not making the change may be much greater.

For example, a university, for excellent business reasons, decides to move its administration building and most of the staff to a neighboring town. They carefully explain the reasons for the move and start the process. Several staff members have long-established family roots in their present locations and have children in the local schools. They have strong attachments to their present location and are not interested in moving for any reason. They are also highly qualified and can find alternative employment. Many of them will not make the transition.

Transformation

The most complex change processes are the transformation processes. The transformation processes involve getting to our core beliefs in our unconscious and making significant life changes. Transformational changes affect our very survival mechanisms and get into the id–the place where our instincts and deepest programming reside. Many modern theorists also link transformation to our center or soul–the place that determines our life purpose and holds our deepest beliefs. This is where our archetypes live and where that special being we call ourselves emanates from.

Transformation change requires all the changes discussed on the previous two levels and then requires changing our reality. Changing reality is only done by conscious choice and only by leaving our present reality. The process is transformational leadership (See the leadership section) and the processes used are those that allow us to see our present reality from a different place. These processes are the unusual or creative processes that may include using art, music, theater, games, guided meditations, outdoor experiences or other creative means to get us into a different place to see where we are and be able to evaluate it.

Will McWhinney uses a simple matrix to give one version of how we might view reality. His matrix is based on looking at our world view in four different ways. The first pair of ways differentiates those who believe the world happens or operates in only one way from those who believe the world operates in many ways. The second pair differentiates those who believe that the world is predetermined and reveals itself from those who believe that the world is based on free choice. Putting the two pairs together creates the following matrix.

	One Way	*Multiple Laws*
Determined	Unitary	Sensory
Free Choice	Mythic	Social

The four realities that are described can be used to understand the process of transformation. The unitary reality has the most difficulty with transformation. People with a unitary reality believe that there is only one determined way to see the world and thus other realities do not exist No transformation can happen with those people until they can be brought to see that other realities exist and that they can choose to believe in them. For example, many scientists have believed that science reveals all answers and that the scientific view is the only way to see the world. They can not stay in that reality and transform their beliefs because they will require scientific proof before they undertake any change. They must be able to escape their scientific prison to see other points of view or other ways of seeing the world. Since other realities don't exist for these scientists, they must be brought to other views through unusual processes that allow them to suspend their present beliefs and play with other realities.

Those with a mythic reality believe there is only one way to see the world and they have chosen or created it. These are the entrepreneurs who create their own views and then expect others to follow them. Many entrepreneurs create very exciting new realities but then become resistant to any changes to their creations. Again, they must be brought out of their current reality to see that other realities exist and that they need to change and can change.

Those with a sensory reality see that there are multiple ways to view the world but believe that the ways are determined by such things as science, religion or perhaps culture. They can change easier than those with only one view of the world but still need to escape their formula for determination to transform.

Those with a social reality are the most open to transformation and are normally those who can lead transformation. They see the world in many ways and can choose among the options that they see. Yet, even those with a social reality must escape their present options and ways of seeing the world to undergo transformation. While it is easiest for those with a social reality, this is a relative term and does not imply it is easy. Transformative change is difficult for individuals and more difficult for groups and organizations.

The three paths of transformation are all different. At the individual level, the process is mentoring. Carl Rogers best described this path in his book, *On Becoming A Person*. He discusses the process of changing another person as the process of engaging with them in a change process and being totally authentic in that process. In other words, to help another person change, I have to be totally open and willing to change and willing to share the essence of myself. The movie *Good Will Hunting* is an example of that process. The therapist had to open and share himself before the other person would trust him and engage in the transformation process. Both the therapist and the client were transformed.

Other processes for individual transformation could include art therapy where the subject can leave their present reality and express their unconscious, or play therapy where the subject can play out their desires or fears. In any case, the process is difficult and normally takes a long time. True transformation normally takes five years (more or less) for the change to take place and be integrated in an individual.

Transformation at the group level is a different process than individual transformation. In this process, the group unconscious is explored and the group purpose, unifying force or beliefs are changed. The group unconscious or group energy is that deep force or set of beliefs that characterize that group, give it an identity and energize the group processes and actions. The group unconscious is similar to Edgar Schein's definition of organization culture. It is the unconscious or hidden beliefs, symbols or mythology that determine the actions of the group.

Transforming a group is a group process and must be done at the group level. Again, the group has a reality similar to the individual reality and the group must escape its current reality to transform. Transforming a group is complicated by the fact that individuals in a group may need to transform for the group to transform. Keeping in mind that individual transformations take about five years to complete, group transformations really cannot accommodate individual transformations unless the group transformation is a very long process.

Group transformations therefore need to be consistent with individual realities or to change the members of the group to adapt to the new group reality. Another way to understand this would be to say that group members must have beliefs similar to the new group beliefs and buy in to the new group culture or leave the group. Groups rarely transform and stay with their same membership.

Organization transformation involves changing the vision, symbols, mythology and collective unconscious of the entire organization or major parts of the organization. Changing the organization culture is normally a transformation. Many organization culture changes have been attempted and few if any have been successfully completed. Transforming the organization means that all or most of the groups will have to transform and large numbers of individuals will need to transform or leave.

The process would be organization wide and involve creating and implementing new shared visions and new beliefs. The organization would have to leave its present reality and adopt a new one. The organization would also have to fit its new reality and culture into whatever indigenous culture exists at all its geographical locations. The process to lead such a change is called transformational leadership. As discussed in the leadership section, transformational leadership includes leadership of spirit, creating the experience of living with heart and drawing on a spiritual force to cut through to a deeper level. These are rare qualities and very deep and personal processes.

Organization transformation is very risky, complicated and difficult. It is also very time consuming and expensive. It should be attempted only as a last resort and when absolutely necessary. ■

Leadership Models

Management of our organizations is very important. Without good management, we don't get excellent short term performance and results. Leadership of our organizations is equally important. Without good leadership, we don't get innovation, change, growth, energy, excitement, vision, collaboration and long term results. Today, when change is constant and innovation is necessary for survival, we must lead our organizations to succeed.

Leadership is an art and a lifelong learning process. There are no shortcuts to becoming a good leader. Leaders are committed to work at it every day. Some characteristics of good leaders that have been observed are:

- Leaders are made, not born.

- Leaders express themselves fully and freely.

- Leaders are passionate about what they do and how they do it.

- Leaders have a lot of energy and energize others.

- Leaders know themselves and are comfortable with who they are.

- Leaders are good listeners and ask good questions.

- Leaders help to create shared visions in their lives and organizations.

- Leaders communicate well to gain cooperation and support.

- Leaders keep their goals clearly in mind and work to achieve them.

- Leaders continue to grow and develop throughout life.

- Leadership is always shared.

- Leaders have strong mentors and mentor others.

- Leaders act from a strong set of deeply felt values.

- Leaders value and respect their people and their relationships.

- Leaders serve their organizations, customers and communities.

- Leaders bring out the best in others.

- Leaders trust others and create an atmosphere of trust.

- Leaders learn to develop and use their intuition.

- Leaders analyze immediate problems and issues from a larger systems perspective.

- Leaders balance short term performance with longer term goals.

- Leaders have a bias for action.

- Leaders strive to act consciously and with integrity.

- Leaders are creative and encourage creativity in others.

- Leaders enjoy what they do and help others to have fun at work.

It is also important to compare management to leadership. Both are important and have their place in the management and running of our organizations. Yet, they are different and are used at different times. The following table may help to differentiate between them.

Leadership	**Management**
Education	Training
Inductive	Deductive
Ideas	Facts
Deep	Surface
Questions	Answers
Process	Content
Strategy	Tactics
Active	Reactive
Whole Brain	Left Brain
Change	Stability
Risk	Rules

There are many books and theories about leadership. One of the best is Warren Bennis's book, *On Becoming a Leader*. This study of successful leaders helps to clearly differentiate the role of leaders and the process of becoming a leader. All leaders agree that they were not born as a leader–they had to do the work to become a leader. Bennis describes the ingredients of leadership as:

1. Vision. Having a guiding vision and a purpose.

2. Integrity. Knowing yourself, candor with yourself and others and maturity based on experience and learning.

3. Instinct. Being independent and following your intuition.

4. Trust. Developing this quality that must be earned.

5. Curiosity. Wondering about everything.

6. Daring. Risk taking and experimenting with new things.

Bennis also defines four competencies of leadership:

1. Managing attention by maintaining a clear vision.

2. Managing meaning through communication of the vision and making it real.

3. Managing trust through integrity, reliability and constancy.

4. Managing yourself through knowing your own strengths and using them.

In organizations with effective leaders, empowerment is most evident in four themes:

1. People feel significant.

2. Learning and competence matter.

3. People are part of a community.

4. Work is exciting.

Abraham Zaleznik of the Harvard Business School argues that managers and leaders are different kinds of people. They differ in motivation, personal history, and how they think and act.

- Managers tend to adopt impersonal, if not passive, attitudes toward goals; where leaders adopt a personal and active attitude toward them.

- Managers tend to view work as an enabling process involving some combination of people and ideas interacting to establish strategies and make decisions. Leaders work from high risk positions, indeed are often temperamentally disposed to seek out risk and danger, especially where opportunity and reward appear high.

- Managers prefer to work with people; they avoid solitary activity because it makes them anxious. They relate to people according to the role they play in a sequence of events or in a decision making process; while leaders, who are concerned with ideas, relate in more intuitive and empathetic ways.

- Managers need order in the face of the potential chaos that many fear in human relationships. In contrast, one often hears leaders referred to in an emotional context. Leaders tend to be people who feel separate from their environment, including other people. They may work in organizations, but they never belong to them. Their sense of who they are doesn't depend on memberships, work roles, or other social indicators of identity.

James Ritscher defines ten qualities of spiritual or transformational leadership. He defines spiritual leadership in two ways:

1. The leadership of spirit in the sense of vitality or depth in an organization and creating the experience of living with heart rather than superficially.

2. Transformational leadership: leadership that draws on a spiritual force and hence cuts through to a deeper level and is thus effective in creating a vital and effective organization.

The ten qualities of spiritual leadership are:

1. Inspired vision

2. Clarity of mind

3. Will, toughness and intention

4. Low ego–high results

5. No separation

6. Trust and openness

7. Insight into human nature

8. Skill in creating people structures–groundedness

9. Integrity

10. A context of personal growth and fulfillment

Willis Harman theorizes that the two main skills needed by modern leaders are:

1. Participatory management

2. Creative/Intuitive leadership

Christopher Meyer summarizes a lot of theory to define the following leadership elements:

1. Connector. Leaders selectively connect people with their own life purpose, spirituality, energy, society, organization resources and vision.

2. Visionary courage. Leaders take risks based on the self-knowledge that mistakes are opportunities, not failures.

3. Letting go. Leaders have the ability to let go of concepts that block new ideas or learning.

4. Balance. Leaders balance action/inaction, praise/correction, change/stability, etc.

5. Competence. Leaders have sufficient expertise and competence to make good judgements and get things done.

The leadership theory can be summarized by combining the elements of leadership into the four "I"s. These are:

Integrity

Involvement

Invention

Initiative

It is appropriate to use "I"s since leadership is essentially personal and reflects ourselves. We become leaders as we work to become leaders. As we master the four "I"s, we become effective leaders. Each element is important on its own and can be learned separately, yet it is the flow of using the four together that truly creates leaders. Each element is discussed.

Integrity

Integrity is the cornerstone of leadership because leaders must be authentic and integrity is the path to authenticity. Integrity is the process of being true to ourselves, which starts with learning to know ourselves and being brutally honest about our talents, skills, thoughts and feelings. We must recognize and develop our strengths and learn to rely on them. We must also be willing to acknowledge and overcome our personal weaknesses. Most of all we must search for and find the truth about ourselves and those we deal with and be willing to express that truth in all our dealings.

Integrity also implies trust and wholeness. Trusting ourselves and our insights, intuition and instincts is very important. Trusting others and their insights and intents is also crucial. As we learn to trust at deeper and deeper levels, we develop wholeness. Wholeness means we bring all of ourselves to our leadership and our work and invite others to do the same.

Integrity also means staying on our path and being constant in what we do. That consistency requires a strong will to achieve defined goals and objectives and a dedication to the shared purpose of the organization. Last, it means that we have mastered the basics of our work so that we can lead others in what we do. We cannot lead what we don't know so we must continually learn and re-learn the basics of our work and our profession.

Involvement

Involvement is the second cornerstone of leadership because leaders must be highly involved in what they are doing and effectively relate and interact with others. This begins with paying attention to our personal commitment to what we are doing. If we are not totally involved in the moment we can't lead. It also means paying attention to our relationships with others, how we interact and what effect we have in our interactions. We learn about our effect on others by paying attention and then asking for feedback.

Involvement also includes the communication, connection, interaction and people orientation that are the basics of working relationships. Leadership is always personal and interpersonal and requires excellent working relationships and human skills. Developing empathy with others is a leadership requisite.

The last piece of involvement is being creative in our leadership and bringing all our creativity to what we do. Creativity involves all our faculties and all our ways of expression. Frequently this means being open to new forms of expression and encouraging others to bring new viewpoints and new approaches to what we do. Making your interactions fun and creative invites others to do the same and energizes the workplace.

Invention

Invention is the third cornerstone of leadership. Leaders invent and re-invent their organizations through bringing visions of where the organization is going and helping to define the overall purpose of the organization. Creating a shared and compelling vision helps organizations to have meaning and gives purpose to the work. Meaningless work is performed routinely and without passion and diminishes the worker. Meaningful work energizes the workforce and promotes creativity and commitment. Leaders help others to find meaning in what they do. Leaders use the shared organization vision to continually remind people how their work fits into the organization purpose and how the organization is serving society.

Invention also includes re-inventing ourselves to remain competent in our profession or skill and to maintain our curiosity about our work. Leaders stimulate themselves and others to continually learn about their field and to expand their competence and their horizons.

Initiative

Initiative is the fourth cornerstone of leadership. The first three areas are internal and interactive qualities. This fourth area is where leaders get into action and movement. Leadership requires we be very active and resourceful and continually move things forward. This bias for action is combined with a tendency to take risks and to act independently. While leaders are very involved in what they do and with their people, they also maintain a level of independence and flexibility so that they can keep things in motion.

Leaders initiate action. They don't wait for others to do something, they find what needs to be done and do it. They are willing to make mistakes and willing to appear foolish at times. They would much rather ask for forgiveness than ask for permission.

Leadership is the opposite of bureaucracy. Leaders continually break the molds that lead toward bureaucracy and frequently find themselves at odds with their organizations. While organizations and managers frequently tend toward stability and control, leaders tend toward change and risk. They maintain enough independence to initiate new actions and keep creativity alive. They are also willing to make mistakes and encourage others to take risks as long as they are learning and moving toward the organization goals. Leaders are also willing to leave organizations when they feel they can no longer be effective. ■

Principles of Change

A start up company wanted to go into a business they knew well and to succeed where others had failed. They then set the company up to do the same things in the same way that they used to do them and were surprised when they failed again.

The leader of an engineering firm knew that the company needed to change and could see that a change in the way the firm was managed would reap great benefits. He also saw that he would have to change and he would need to add value in new ways. The fear of not being needed was greater than the perceived benefits. No change took place.

Change is hard. Most businesses talk about change but have great difficulty in actually changing direction or how things are done. Some principles of implementing change:

- Change should start and end with the customer.
- Innovation is a key ingredient of change.
- Change happens through people.
- Leadership is necessary to implement change.
- Change requires a sense of urgency.
- Change requires courage.
- Effective change must be planned and the results measured.

- Major change involves reconstructing reality.

- Change requires a critical mass supporting it to gain commitment.

- Change requires excellent communication in all directions.

- Effective change requires a shared vision of the desired state.

- Change is a process.

- Change is incremental.

- Only so much change can happen at one time.

- Change takes a lot of energy.

- To change my business, I must change.

A large state agency decided their divisions needed to change and started a major program to implement teams. The teams were formed and wanted the authority to make decisions. The top managers were unwilling to release control. No effective change happened.

If you really want to change your business, be prepared to make a major effort, follow the principles and stick with it. Your leadership is absolutely essential to successful change. ■

Discussion Questions:

1. Are you really willing to change? What are you willing to change?

2. Have your past change efforts been successfully implemented? Why not?

Outrageous Managers are willing to change themselves.

Transformation– Terra Incognita

*T*ransformation change is truly the journey into the unknown or what early maps of the world would call "terra incognita". When we left the known and charted world, we went into the unknown world. Most change models call for unfreezing the existing system, making necessary changes and then re-freezing the new changes. That model works fine for simple change and most transitions. It will not work for transformation.

The model for transformation change is to leave our present reality, enter the void and then emerge into a new reality. The introduction to this chapter discussed the use of wild and unusual processes to leave our present realities. The decision to leave our present reality usually happens only when some disaster has happened or our business is threatened with bankruptcy or some other major calamity. The decision to transform is always a choice. Even faced with extinction, many companies will not choose to leave their present reality. The fear of the unknown can be stronger than the will to survive. For those who make the choice, the crisis precipitates taking the critical first step–leaving the known world.

The difficult and murky part of the journey is the decision to enter the void–terra incognita. Entering the void means leaving the linear and rational world behind and embracing the unknown. In mythology, this is the hero's journey, the grail quest, the adventure to slay the dragon. It is also the inward journey. The inward journey takes us into the void, the abyss, the black hole within ourselves where we face our deepest fears and either conquer them or become devoured by them. Yet it is only through the darkness and terror of the void that we find the light–the message of transformation.

In transformation, our individual construction of reality is changed. In organization transformation, our social construction of reality is changed as well. We may find ourselves back in the same place we started but we are not the same people and see that place in a totally different way. In 1987, I entered a doctoral program at The Fielding Institute and was required to write an autobiography. I titled it New Beginnings because my life was characterized by several key transformations that were precipitated by major disasters and led to major internal changes.

The disasters were major to me–fighting in Vietnam, divorce, a mid-life existential crisis and the death of my oldest son. The changes and growth were profound and each of them took a long time and a lot of pain. My reality and world view changed with each transformation and yet I have been an organization consultant and change agent through all the changes. I came back to the same place but in totally new ways and with a whole new perspective. The form has stayed the same–the substance and meaning were totally altered. The journey is a spiral path. As Yogi Berra would say, it's deja vu all over again.

The journey through the void is an absolutely necessary part of the process of transformation. Be willing to face your demons, beliefs, structures, ego, and identity. Be open to listen to your inner voice that will guide the journey. It is only through surrender to the journey and embracing the darkness that we find the courage and wisdom to re-emerge–transformed into new people and organizations doing things in new ways. ■

Discussion Questions:

1. Are you willing to enter terra incognita–the unknown?

2. Does your organization have the courage to face its deepest fears?

Outrageous Managers embrace the unknown.

Technology Change

A national retail company automated all their stores and put in all new systems. They didn't change their management approach and received no return on their new technology.

A large chemical company automated many of their manufacturing and inventory processes. The people involved never embraced the technology and continued to run their manual systems.

Technology change is a special type of systems change or transition. As we move into the information age, new technology seems to be appearing everywhere and it is assumed that all new technology is good and should be installed immediately. Designing and implementing new technology is actually a major transition in most organizations and one that changes many different aspects of how a business is managed and operated. Few major technology changes happen easily and many never get implemented.

The decision to significantly change technology is a decision to significantly change the organization, the management systems and the careers of the people involved. New technology may also involve changing many of the formal and informal social structures of the organization and involve layoffs, reassignments or transfers. New technology also affects the skills necessary for many people in the organization and may affect the prevailing culture. In any case, new technology is a major change and all the factors need to be planned for successful implementation—not just the technology changes.

As with any transition, the change process involves dealing with the mental systems and emotional systems that determined our present behavior. These processes take time, leadership and commitment. We can not simply demand transitions or manage them in a top down way. Those involved must be included in the process and led through the change processes. Transition always involves choice. The reasons to make the transition must be compelling to those involved and their motivation to change must be greater than their reasons for not changing or leaving.

Technology transitions also involve major system changes. Changing the technology also frequently means making major changes in:

- Business processes. The ways that we actually conduct all the business that the technology will affect.

- Management systems. The approach to managing the business and the ways that we manage, plan, operate and measure the business results.

- Systems or management systems for all those who interact with the affected technology, including other company functions (such as finance, accounting and marketing), suppliers, customers and support groups.

- Management teams. The composition, structure, roles and prevailing values may need to change on several different levels of management teams.

Technology change is a major transition. It will take a minimum of a year and more likely two to three years to complete the process. Make the decision to change wisely and then commit the time, the resources and the leadership to make it happen. Enjoy the journey. ■

Discussion Questions:

1. Who makes your technology change decisions? Are they implemented?

2. Are you getting the benefits from new technology? Why not?

Outrageous Managers lead technology change.

Failure To Implement

A *well established manufacturing company experienced slumping sales and severe cash flow issues. They developed a turnaround plan with three action steps. Six months later, little had been accomplished and the company was struggling for survival.*

A nutritional products startup company was well funded by venture capitalists, had great products and had an exciting marketing plan. The management teamed failed to execute the key elements of their sales and marketing strategies. The business failed, the venture capitalists lost six million dollars and the management team felt defeated.

A successful toy company is now in year four of a well thought out five year business plan. They have attempted to consistently execute the key elements of their plan, sometimes with more success than others. This management team walked their talk and implemented their plans. Their company is growing and very profitable.

Troubled companies do not generally fail by surprise. Their ailments are known and the outcomes are predictable. Companies do not miss their sales or profitability numbers for lack of good ideas. Frequently companies do not achieve their goals because they fail to implement the plans they have created.

Companies and the people within them are similar to supertankers, they can take a long time to change direction even when a new course is desired. But if you physically turn the wheel, the rudder will move and ship will alter its course. Similarly, action within your business will produce results. Successful change requires planning, execution, monitoring results, and making small but consistent corrections along the way. A few major course corrections may be required. If your company is stuck, knows and talks about the solutions but fails to implement them, then there are unspoken or unresolved issues that are causing the blockage. If you are ready to move forward, consider asking yourself and your management team the following questions:

- Do we really agree on the root cause of our problems? Or the potential opportunity?

- Do we truly believe that the plans we have outlined are doable and realistic?

- Why are we placing our resources (time, money, people) on lower priority tasks?

- Who are we protecting in our company? Are we ignoring performance, capability or accountability issues?

- What sacred cows (traditions, practices, beliefs) are alive and well in our company that no longer serve us well?

- How can we hold ourselves accountable for our actions?

These are difficult questions. The answers may be even tougher. Your company's success depends on it. Take the risk, ask the questions and move forward. Make implementation a positive force in forging your business success. ■

Discussion Questions:

1. What three things continually block implementation of new initiatives? What will you do
about them?

2. Who helps get new initiatives implemented?
Who gets in the way? What action is required?

Outrageous Managers are tenacious about implementation.

How To Use A Consultant

A large company hires a consultant to write their new strategic plan. The consultant does an excellent job and writes a wonderful plan but it goes on a shelf and no one uses it. The money and effort are wasted.

Another large company hires consultant after consultant to define what is wrong and fix the company. The consultants do their best but no change takes place and the company, managers and employees are frustrated. Top management really doesn't want to change.

A board of directors brings in a large consulting company to restructure the company. They spend a lot of money and change a lot of people but don't achieve long term financial improvement and lose several key people.

As a business consultant for 30 years, I have developed some ideas about how to best use consultants to get the most for your business. Here are some approaches and observations that may help:

- You are the expert in your business–the consultant is not the expert in your business. Consultants are catalysts who help you lead change and manage your business better.

- If you don't want to change, don't hire a consultant. Too many clients hire consultants to help them change their business but don't really want to change. Changes in your business will require you to change. Really–you will have to change.

- Rarely does a consulting engagement follow the path that is defined in a contract. In most cases, the initially defined scope of work is only a symptom or indicator of the work required. Defining the problem or opportunity is part of the work. Be open to the path and the process.

- Consulting is an interactive relationship. Work with consultants you trust and who communicate well with you. It takes trust and time to share the truth about ourselves and our business. The benefit received is directly proportional to the quality of the relationship and our ability to discuss the truth about ourselves and our business.

- Hire the person you want to work with, not the firm.

- Consultants have frequently been successful when you think you didn't need them at the end of the engagement. That means that you have taken ownership of the ideas and processes that have been recommended and they will be implemented.

- Consulting engagements are most effective when the key client managers work with the consultant and stay involved in the process. Dedicate time to the process.

- Short summary reports of engagements are normally helpful reminders and serve to crystallize the thinking and results of the process. Long reports gather dust.

- Consultants are catalysts of change. Hire the consultant who matches the type and level of change that is required.

- Consulting and the consulting process take time and effort–yours and the consultant's. Don't expect quick fixes or easy answers. Commit to the process and expect to expend reasonable levels of effort, money and time.

Consultants are trusted advisors who can be objective, stimulating, honest, wise, and knowledgeable. Consultants can be mentors, catalysts, analysts, observers, coaches, technical experts, facilitators, designers, friends and confidants. Consultants are dedicated to making you and your business more successful.

Discussion Questions:

1. Do you have the courage to discuss problems and issues with your own management team? Is it easier to hear bad news from strangers?

2. Act as your own consultant. What is wrong with the business? What would you change? Can you lead the changes?

Outrageous Managers partner with their consultants.

Kill Bureaucracy Before It Kills You

*A*top executive goes into public service to revamp the procurement and logistics functions of the Department of
Defense. After four years of hard work he concludes
that he has had little or no effect on changing the existing
processes and methods.

A remote mining company experiences very high turnover
so they add more layers and backup positions. Turnover
increases, overhead skyrockets and productivity drops.

A manufacturer engineers procedures to control every step
of the production process. The jobs become mindless, several key
people leave and profits drop substantially.

These are all cases of bureaucracy. Bureaucracy is
defined as specialization of functions, adherence to
fixed rules, inflexible routine, extensive red tape and a
hierarchy of authority. It permeates all businesses to
some degree. The characteristics of bureaucracy are an
obsession with control, depersonalization of work,
dependency of the worker on the supervisor, a patriarchal contract, a machine metaphor and placing a
high value on obedience. The results are the stifling of
initiative, the death of creativity, an inability to adapt
and change, the sapping of the energy of the workforce and a dreary place to work. None of us likes
working in those conditions, so why does bureau-

cracy continue to show up and take root in our businesses? Fear! Our individual and collective fears do us in.

Here are just a few of the assumptions and fears that lead us to let bureaucracy creep in:

- Fear of failure/making a mistake. Doing nothing is better than being wrong.

- Fear of looking bad. Status is more important than results.

- Fear of not being good enough. I have to be the smartest, best, most successful, etc.

- Fear of rejection/closeness. If they really knew me they would not like me.

- Fear of autonomy. Freedom leads to chaos and ruin.

- Fear of not fitting in. If I'm different or stand out, I'll be ostracized.

- Fear of others. People are out to get me/I really don't belong here.

We all have some of these or other fears at work. Don't feel alone but don't act on them either. One key to eliminating mindless bureaucracy is to acknowledge the fear, share it out loud and then move through it. The most amazing thing normally happens when we share what we are feeling with others–yes, even at work. Other workers or managers are normally feeling the same thing and become excited about getting it out and moving on. The fear loses its power! Unexpressed fear keeps us imprisoned and gives others control over us. Expressed fear loses its power and fades away. Control is only an illusion.

We defeat bureaucracy when we energize ourselves and others in the business and develop the courage to be unique, create, be real, have fun, speak truth, relate to others, take risks, make mistakes, act autonomously, make conscious decisions, and generally enjoy the journey. Bashing bureaucracy is a popular business sport–it is also a difficult and challenging journey that leads to professional and business growth, creativity and success. ■

Discussion Questions:

1. What are the fears that permeate your organization? Do you feel stifled and controlled? What will you do about it?

2. What are the positive benefits of bureaucracy in your business? What are the negative effects? What will you do about it?

Outrageous Managers kill bureaucracy before it spreads.

You Know That You're a Bureaucrat When...

1. You spend all day in meetings, most of which plan other meetings.

2. You fit all the people you know into neat little boxes.

3. You worry a lot about getting more people reporting to you.

4. You agonize over decisions that mean very little.

5. You believe your business centers around you.

6. You can't answer your kids when they ask you what you do.

7. You believe that people really care about your opinions about everything.

8. You know that only you can really make a good decision.

9. You believe that everyone who works for you is there to serve you.

10. You lie awake at night knowing that *they* are out to get you.

11. You think that playing golf or drinking with the boys (girls) is really doing business.

12. You believe that committees actually do something.

13. You spend more and more time defining new perks.

14. You believe that morale depends on your personal happiness.

15. You hoard information because others don't need to know.

16. You believe that your primary responsibility is to protect those above and below you.

17. You believe that your boss is the customer you need to serve.

18. You practice the golden rule of going along to get along.

19. You are always too busy to deal with real business problems.

20. You have your secretary constantly tell people that you are tied up in meetings.

21. You believe you really are entitled to make that much more than your subordinates.

22. You are the only one to speak at a staff meeting.

23. You haven't paid for your own lunch since you got your present job.

24. You were hired based on your friendships and country club membership.

25. You control access to your office tighter than the FBI.

26. You are insulted when someone actually does something without giving you credit.

27. You believe that the way things have always been done is obviously the best.

28. You believe that policies and procedures actually drive actions.

29. You continually say 'Don't fix it if it ain't broke'.

30. You spend endless hours reworking and increasing your fictitious budget.

31. You actually start to believe your own budget numbers.

32. You believe that further analysis is always preferable to action.

33. You avoid decisions at all costs because they would make you accountable.

34. You spend time studying those above you so you can dress and act like them.

35. You believe that the measly raises and perks you give out actually buy loyalty.

36. You immediately blame others for any errors or problems and focus only on the blame.

37. You ignore or bury any bad news about your business.

38. You delay and analyze any new programs until they go away.

39. You personally make all presentations so that you get the credit.

40. You rework your organization charts constantly and believe that will fix things.

41. You hire people based on their admiration for you and if they make you feel good.

42. You know that your business could never run without you. ■

Discussion Questions:

1. How have you become a bureaucrat? Is that a surprise?

2. Are you willing to take the risks to act freely and independently?

Outrageous Managers hate bureaucracy.

Business Turnarounds

A national retail company suffers through slowly diminishing profits and reduced investor confidence. They bring in a new management team to turn the company around but fail to get the support of the employees or the board and they fail.

A Fortune 500 industrial company expands into new areas and new businesses to turn around falling revenues and profits. They don't understand the new businesses and fail.

A manufacturing company is experiencing declining market shares and margins and decides to re-engineer to turn things around. They fail to implement and decline.

Most companies periodically face the prospect of needing to turn around some aspect of their business. Unfortunately, we are normally not very good at this. The situations that require us to go into a turnaround mode usually indicate that we are performing poorly and under severe stress. Something is not working well and needs correction. What is it?

Defining what needs to be fixed is the first step and a crucial one. Many companies go into action too quickly and follow the fire, ready, aim model. Carefully planning the turnaround and defining the issues that need redirection can prevent solving the wrong problem and yield very positive results. Getting your teams and key people involved in defining the issues and approach can significantly help in getting the results implemented.

The need for a turnaround is a symptom that calls for a return to the basics and applications of innovation and leadership. To effectively change direction requires reviewing and assessing the current status of our planning, process and performance, and then defining the changes in those key elements that will get the business back on track. Successfully leading a turnaround is a chance to redirect, refocus and re-energize the business.

There are three major dangers in a turnaround process. The first is that the same people who are running the company define the turnaround–this leads back to doing the same things you were doing before without effective change. The second danger is throwing out too much and losing the key success factors that kept the business going. A combination of external consultants and internal staff can help prevent both errors. The third major danger is taking too long. Set aggressive goals for the turnaround and stick to them. Implementation of the turnaround should be underway within two months.

Business turnarounds can be an opportunity to get down to the core issues that are facing a company and to redirect the business on the road to success. The business basics checklist will help you focus on what is not working and what are the core issues that need to be addressed. Making the necessary changes and course corrections will ensure that you get the desired outcome–a business that is achieving profits and results. ■

Discussion Questions:

1. Do you have the courage to make the changes necessary to turn around your business or area?

2. Are you clear on what changes need to be made? How do you know?

Outrageous Managers courageously turn around their business.

Chapter 3
Energizing Relationships And Teams

Managers spend most of their time communicating with people. There are new people we meet from time to time but most management communications are with people we know well–our colleagues, team members, staff, suppliers, advisors, key customers and other regular members of our community. These regular community members are those with whom we have developed–or not developed–working relationships. Working relationships are an absolute key to business success and yet we normally pay little attention to them. These relationships are seen as the "soft" or "process" side of business.

Studies have shown that 85% of those leaving an organization do so because of failed working relationships–not performance issues. Many businesses also fail because the working relationships of the key people didn't work. There is nothing "soft" about creating and maintaining successful working relationships. Our working relationships are the process side of business–

the side that determines whether we want to go to work in the morning, whether we are motivated or perfunctory, whether we are creative or machine like, whether we relate to others in a way that energizes people and makes them want to be around us.

When other people want to work with us, we are energizing our working relationships. When people want to avoid us or interact only out of necessity, we are de-energizing our working relationships and courting disaster. Energizing our working relationships and teams shows up on the bottom line both personally and professionally. De-energizing them is also very clear on the bottom line—failed relationships create a black hole for our organizational energy and our business profits.■

Working Relationships Models

Paying attention to working relationships is as important and sometimes as difficult as our personal relationships. Organization is all about successful relationships. So, how do we go about developing successful working relationships? It's not easy and yet there are some principles that may help:

- Clearly define the purpose and specific goals of the relationship up front.

- Measure the benefits of the relationship in terms of results.

- Open and honest communication is essential.

- Actively listen and make sure you understand the meaning of what is said.

- Acknowledge and celebrate differences.

- Accept that relationships are difficult and that you are at least half of the problem.

- Assume good intentions and develop trust until proven otherwise.

- Promote positive conflict and solve negative conflicts.

- Pay more attention to actions than words–your own and others.

- Work toward win–win solutions and relationships.

Research has shown that if no one is paying attention to the relationship, then the parties will not be happy and the relationship will eventually fail. Relationships work best when both parties are paying attention, however we can only take responsibility for our own actions. So it is critical that we pay attention to our relationships with investors, suppliers, parents, team members, alliances and others we work with to achieve success.

There are not a lot of books written on working relationships. Working relationships are similar to friendships but have a different purpose. Working relationships are also similar to personal relationships but have a different purpose and operate at a different level. We don't need to love our co-workers and others we relate to at work. We do need to get along and achieve the goals that caused the relationship to be defined. This isn't easy.

There are four factors that appear to be necessary to have successful working relationships. These are the four "A"s of working relationships and we need to get an A in each of them to be successful. They are:

Attraction. Defining the purpose that brought you together.

Attention. Communicating and relating in ways that are effective.

Attachment. Commitment to making the relationship work.

Action. Doing what was agreed and achieving the desired results.

Pulling from work done in many fields, each of these areas will be discussed below.

Attraction

In personal relationships, we are more likely to be attracted to someone if that person:

1. Has similar beliefs, values and personality characteristics

2. Satisfies our needs

3. Is physically attractive

4. Is pleasant or agreeable

5. Reciprocates our liking and

6. Is in geographical proximity to us

Working relationships adhere to the principles of social exchange. Reciprocity is the rule in these relationships: what one gives to such relationships and what one gets are kept in balance. Whereas participants in an exchange relationship are more likely to keep track of contributions and to reciprocate in kind, participants in communal relationships are more likely to be tuned to the other person's needs.

Interdependence is the hallmark of working relationships. We compare the costs to the rewards and we also compare the present working relationship to a subjective standard. This comparison is based on past experiences and we judge the present working relationship to be successful only if it exceeds the comparison level. The comparison level can change over time. As you grow older you may demand more from a relationship than you did when you were younger. We also compare new alternatives to our present working relationships. If a present working relationship is working well, we are less likely to look for new alternatives. If the present working relationship is not going well, we are more likely to be open to new alternatives and to change or end the existing relationship.

Subjective evaluations are very important in the social exchange process. Rewards and costs are not objective standards that can be measured with a ruler. Rather, they depend on individual beliefs, on attributions about ourselves and others, and they are subject to constant change.

Attraction thus defines the purpose for the relationship and its basis. While we may or may not be physically, emotionally or mentally attracted to those we work with, we need to have some basis for the relationship or it will not last. The rational goals are one part of why we work together but they will not be sufficient to keep a working relationship going. We must find the subjective reasons for the relationship as well and define the similarities or other attractions that make the relationship important.

We can do a lot to help make a working relationship attractive by exploring beliefs and values, defining and meeting the other person's needs, being pleasant, acting reciprocally and spending time together.

Attention

Interpersonal intelligence is the ability to understand other people; what motivates them, how they work, and how to work cooperatively with them. Intrapersonal intelligence is the correlative ability turned inward. It is the capacity to form an accurate model of oneself and to be able to use that model to operate effectively in life. Effective working relationships require that we not only develop both forms of intelligence, but that we use them. We must apply what we know about ourselves and other people to make our relationships work. In other words, we must pay attention to the relationships and nurture them.

Hatch and Gardner have identified the four key components of interpersonal intelligence:

1. Organizing Groups. The essential skill of the leader, this involves initiating and coordinating the efforts of a network of people.

2. Negotiating Solutions. The talent of the mediator, preventing conflicts or resolving those that flare up.

3. Personal Connection. The empathy and connecting that make it easy to enter into an encounter or to recognize and respond fittingly to people's feelings and concerns–the art of relationship.

4. Social Analysis. The ability to detect and have insights about other people's feelings, motives and concerns that leads to an easy intimacy and a sense of rapport.

Paying attention also includes effective communication. To relate to someone else, we need to communicate in ways that they can hear and understand and also in ways that they feel good about the process. We can be very clear in what we have to say and destroy the relationship through the way we say it. Paying attention means being sensitive to the other persons needs and trying to meet them.

We also need to understand our own needs and express them effectively. We cannot expect others to meet our needs if they don't know what they are and how they can succeed. When our needs or the other person's needs don't get met, we then need to deal with the apparent conflict. Several articles on conflict outline the differences between positive and negative conflict and present models for resolving conflicts when they arise.

Attachment

Attachment is the positive affective bond (usually invisible) that is formed between two (or more) people in a relationship. In working relationships, the bond is usually more of an affiliation than an attachment. Affiliations are a weaker type of bond that are both less secure and less demanding. The origins of attachment theory come from examining the bond between an infant and the mother or primary care giver. Those bonds are very strong and the survival of the infant depends on the care provided.

For working relationships, the keys are the positive affects that we create with the other person. A strictly mental or rational relationship is normally defined by a contract and has no affective or emotional content. These rational relationships rarely exist in actuality and rarely work because they leave out the human and personal factors.

Psychologists have coined the word alexithymia to describe people who are unable to express emotion. That describes how people have been in the work place for a long time. They feel what is going on but have been told to suppress it or ignore it. Of course the feelings were still there and the people acted on them but never expressed them. This created a confusing and chaotic workplace because the emotions were hidden and repressed but still determined actions and outcomes.

Most of our working relationships have also suffered from alexithymia. We have feelings about the relationship but they stay unexpressed. It is very important to acknowledge those feelings and express them to form the attachments necessary for healthy working relationships. If we can't find and express a positive affective reason for the relationship then the relationship will probably wither and die. We need to find a connection, a bond. Relationships are personal and we need to find the personal attachment to commit to them and make them work.

Action

Without action, there is no working relationship. This is the rational part of the working relationship that ensures that the agreed upon actions take place and the results are achieved. Effective action in working relationships requires:

1. Clearly defined goals

2. Action to meet the goals

3. Measurement of the results

4. Discussion and follow up

Spending time at the beginning of a working relationship to clearly define the expected outcomes and results is critical. More working relationships fail because of unclear goals and expectations than for any other reason. Put the goals in writing and make sure both people have reviewed them and agree. The process of writing them on paper always leads to greater clarity. Where appropriate, include specific action steps, deadlines, costs and other critical factors. Defining desired methods and levels of communication is also helpful.

Measurement and follow up are an important part of the process. The KISS theory is the most important part of any successful measurement program–keep it simple stupid! A few principles that may help are outlined in the article on performance measurement.

To summarize, successful working relationships require that we get an A in four key areas: Attraction, Attention, Attachment and Action. We need to define the purpose for the relationship and find the balance and common values that make it attractive. We need to pay attention to the working relationship and apply our interpersonal intelligence. We want to find the affective bond that attaches us to the other person. And we want to act on the purpose that created the working relationship and accomplish the desired results. Getting an A in each area leads to an excellent working relationship. ■

Team Development Models

Many authors have described "The Myth Of The Management Team". They describe the management team as a myth because it is so rare and seldom truly emerges It is easy to describe and remember management teams that did not work. Those teams that did work truly are outrageous and accomplished goals that did not seem attainable. The remarkable thing about the successful teams is that they appeared ordinary. There were no super stars, there was no great new theory they used, they were not geniuses, there was no charismatic leader, and at first they didn't appear to be that good. What made them outrageous was what they accomplished, not what they appeared to be.

These outrageous teams had some similar characteristics, including:

- The teams were results oriented and they held each other strictly accountable.

- The members of the team were able to be themselves–they brought their talent, humor, failings, ideas, experience, insights, and personalities to the team.

- The team leader was open and willing to share that leadership–it was frequently hard to define who was in charge.

- The team had fun together and were able to celebrate successes, grieve over failures, laugh at themselves and share the experiences of their organization and their lives.

- The team was very focused on their plans and performance and accomplished a lot of work individually and collectively.

- They were people oriented–they seemed to enjoy each other and the diverse points of view each member could bring. They respected and valued their differences.

- They had a tolerance of ambiguity and chaos–they were direct with each other, encouraged disagreement and challenged assumptions and statements.

- They were creative and able to think and act out of the box.

- They were accountable–they did what they said they would do and did not tolerate missed deadlines and poor quality work. They were specific on action items, followed up at every meeting to review what had been done and what or who needed help.

There is no magic formula for successful management teams. They just work hard, concentrate on change, be themselves, respect each other and demand top quality performance and results.

Team development, or what has been traditionally called team building, falls generally within the fields of organization development, organization psychology and social psychology. Organization development consists of a planned process of change through the utilization of behavioral models, research and theory, and is normally practiced through use of the action research method. The field of organization psychology started as the psychological study of individuals in the workplace and has grown into an interdisciplinary field reflecting the growing interest of psychologists, sociologists, anthropologists, political scientists, system theorists and others in attempting to understand organizational phenomena. Social psychology focuses on human social interaction, exploring all the ways in which our behaviors affect and are affected by other people. Other fields also affect the behavior of teams.

Teams operate in a very complex and still poorly understood environment. The following guidelines or insights were distilled from some of the key theorists and pioneers in each field.

A lot of the work in the field of organization development derives from the efforts of Kurt Lewin. Lewin viewed the organization as a dynamic social system with many varied subsystems, primarily groups. Individuals will more readily accept changes when the group changes and the restraining forces are reduced. Lewin also differentiates between imposed forces, those acting on a person from the outside, and a person's own forces that come from within and reflect our own needs. A person will naturally follow and accomplish goals that come from within while they may be highly resistant to goals set by others unless they match their own internal goals or they are constantly influenced/monitored.

Social psychology helps us understand the dynamics of people working in groups vs working alone. Human beings are complex social animals with social needs that affect how we behave around others. The processes of interaction or non-interaction, higher or lower performance, comfort, commitment and many others are affected by how the individuals socialize in a group and how the individual's needs and goals reflect those of the group. There are also many other variables, including group size, communication networks, roles and expectations, the nature of group tasks, characteristics of individual members and others.

Organization psychology overlaps quite a bit with the fields of organization development and social psychology. It does add some research and theory to how groups work specifically in an organizational environment. Specifically, it adds some insights into how to use groups in organizations and how to train organization members to be better group members and better accomplish the organization objectives.

The process of team building, which is now called team development to reflect its ongoing nature has been around for over 25 years but really began to proliferate in the 1970s and 1980s. Some observations from the team building sources are summarized below.

- Team development should begin with a strongly felt need to improve some basic condition or process that is interfering with the achievement of organizational goals.

- The underlying reason for starting a team development program should be clear evidence of a lack of effective teamwork.

- Team development can be envisioned as a process of getting work-unit members together and involving them in a total program of problem solving and development.

- Some cautions in team building: Team building takes time; people in power must support changes; involvement enhances commitment; team development may need to be done more than once; and team building must be rewarded.

- Team development does not mean managing by committee, where no one is in charge and all actions must be decided by all.

- Teams continually go through the four stages of development in learning to interact with each other: forming; storming; norming; and performing.

- Several conditions must exist before effective teams can be developed:

  1) The group must have a natural reason for working together that makes sense

  2) The members of the group must be mutually dependent on one another's experience, abilities, and commitment in order to fulfill mutual objectives

  3) Group members must be committed to the idea that working together as a group, rather than in isolation or opposition, leads to more effective decisions, and

  4) The group must be accountable as a functioning unit within a larger organizational context.

Team building works when four conditions are met:

  1) Interdependence. The team is working on important problems in which each person has a stake. Team work is essential to success, not an ideology or an ought-to;

  2) Leadership. The boss wants to improve performance so strongly they will take risks;

  3) Joint Decision. All members agree to participate; and

  4) Equal Influence. Each person has a chance to influence the agenda.

- Companies with strong performance standards spawn more real teams than companies that promote teams per se.

- High-performance teams are extremely rare. Much of the wisdom of teams lies in the disciplined pursuit of performance.

- By focusing on performance and team basics, as opposed to trying to become a team, most small groups can deliver the performance results that require team behavior.

Summarizing the team development theory can be done by looking at the four stages of development and the four "co"s of team development. The stages of development are:

- Forming

- Storming

- Norming

- Performing

To simplify the theory of team development, the theory has been summarized into four "co"s. The term "co" is appropriate because everything to do with team success is shared and the prefix "co" means jointly or together. The four "co"s of team development are:

Commitment

Cooperation

Composition

Contribution

Commitment

Commitment starts with the personal purpose and the team purpose. When each individual's purpose aligns with and supports the group or team purpose, then commitment begins. Commitment provides the energy that helps the team get through the tough process of surrendering individual egos to the higher team purpose or mission.

Without commitment, individual goals dominate and the team goals don't get completed. Teams are always formed for a purpose and the process of development moves them toward the ability to effectively accomplish that purpose. A key part of team formation is defining the specific team goals, the tasks that will be accomplished and how the achievement of those goals or tasks will be measured. Commitment to a team includes both the commitment to the team process and the commitment to accomplish the assigned goals and tasks. Without commitment to the goals and tasks, the team process becomes circular and meaningless.

Cooperation

The second "co" of teams is cooperation. Cooperation is the necessary ingredient to get a team through the storming phase. Cooperation includes the ability to communicate effectively, the trust necessary to work together, the interdependence to flow individual and team processes and efforts, and the feedback processes to help team members understand their impact on others.

Cooperation also includes the use of positive conflict and the resolution of negative conflicts. The storming phase of development usually also involves questions of leadership. Learning to cooperate is a necessary ingredient for shared leadership. Shared leadership means that each team member will lead those areas of the team goals and tasks in which they are expert or competent. Without shared leadership, there is no team–there are just a group of people doing a task under the supervision of a manager. An essential concept of being a team is that we each contribute uniquely and cooperate so that the whole is larger than the sum of the parts.

Composition

The third "co" of leadership is composition. Team composition refers to the team size, skills and diversity that allow it to succeed. Teams that are too large usually cannot develop the cooperation necessary to move from storming to norming. Those that are too small cannot complete the assigned tasks because they lack necessary skills or the diversity to be creative and effective. Teams establish norms and start working on their tasks when they feel confident and can start seeing how they will accomplish their goals and tasks. The necessary skills and diversity are critical.

Diversity lets us differentiate which tasks and goals each team member can bring. If all the team members are similar, then group think or infighting will occur. It is the diversity that makes a team special and allows it to be creative and effective. Divergent backgrounds, skills, styles, personalities, levels, and other factors give a team its richness and potential.

Contribution

The fourth "co" of teams is their contribution. The contribution of the team is the problems it solves, the decisions made, the actions completed and the results accomplished. A team that gets along but doesn't contribute is a failure. A team that accomplishes its goals and achieves excellent results is a success. Concentration on the goals and contributions is usual a great key to team success. ■

Energizing Your Business

More and more business articles are being written about creativity, leadership, intuition, empowerment, community, co-creation, team spirit, culture, transformation, healing, integrity, ethics, new science, quantum physics, learning, development, self-renewing systems and many other topics that we view as the "soft" side of business. Why are they being written and what do they really mean for us and our businesses?

In the business world of chaos, white water, constant change and continuous learning and creativity, the old answers don't seem to work any more. We are searching for meaning in our business lives and the old paradigms of a machine-based, materialistic world don't give it to us. We want to be passionate about what we do and work with high energy people who share our passions. We want to feel energized and make a difference.

Business has a new role in society. Business is where we spend most of our time, where most of our relationships take place and where we look for meaning and value in our lives. Social change has become almost synonymous with changes in our economy and our businesses. We have moved away from the world where the different aspects of our lives were separate and distinct. We defined ourselves in clear roles and definitions. Now, nothing is quite clear. We are being asked to bring all of ourselves to work, to our relationships and to our community. The distinctions between our home life, our work life and our communities are dimming. We are being asked to act consciously in all our relationships. We are being asked to energize our businesses and our communities.

So, how do we energize our businesses and achieve this sense of purpose and meaning?

- Dare to be yourself.

- Commit to lifelong learning and development.

- Be open to new ways of seeing and doing things.

- Look inside for answers. Develop and use your intuition.

- Find your own purpose and then pursue it.

- Do what you are good at and what you enjoy doing.

- Make conscious choices.

- Make decisions based on values and principles rather than rules.

- Organize based on relationships and abilities rather than structures and boxes.

- Work through your fears. Get help when needed.

- Pay attention to your body, your mind, your gut instincts and other irrational inputs.

- Let loose your imagination, creativity, dreams and sense of wonder.

- Be autonomous and act freely based on courage and conviction.

- Dare to be great.

- Respect others and honor their differences.
- Take time for reflection and introspection–connect with nature.
- Find and bring out the special qualities and abilities of others.
- View your business and career as a journey and enjoy the ride.
- Empower and encourage others to do the same. ■

Discussion Questions:

1. Do you add energy to your business or sap it? Are you sure?
2. What three things will you do to energize yourself and your business? When?

Outrageous Managers energize their communities.

Putting "U" Back In Your BSiness

*T*he leader of a growing business takes on more and more administrative tasks to help the business survive and grow. Eventually she discovers that she has no time to create new products and market them to customers—the reason she started the business. She runs out of energy and the business declines.

A highly creative entrepreneur wants to finance his business growth so he prepares a logical business plan. His vision and his personal goals are unclear and the banker turns down his loan. The banker explains that anyone can start a business but only those that have passion and a clear vision are likely to work through the hard times and succeed.

An excellent engineer loves the challenge of difficult design problems and thrives on technical detail. He is promoted to manager of the division and everyone suffers.

The administrative age of business was based on the principle that work is impersonal. Managers and workers were to do exactly what they were told and obedience and loyalty were the prized attributes. Most of us have moved forward to more creative and personal approaches to work and yet many businesses still retain many elements or practices that reflect the impersonal or bureaucratic assumptions and principles. We can all walk into a business and know almost immediately if the people there are excited about what they do and committed to their goals and success. We most assuredly know when the people are negative and perfunctory. We don't want to do business with flat, remote people.

Let's be honest, most of us have parts of business that we love and are very good at and other parts that bore us to tears and we do reluctantly and slowly. Luckily, we are all different and the jobs that bore me are the jobs someone else dreams about. When I work on the jobs that are boring to me, I am not doing myself or the business any good. This usually happens when someone tells me I should be good at this, or that if I'm a team player I will share in these undesirable tasks. Somewhere the notion that we are all the same was equated with the notion of being equal. To me, equality means that we are all able to pursue what we are passionate about and to contribute based on our abilities and talents. I do best for myself and the business when I follow my passion and my dreams.

Businesses also have dreams and passions. When people who share a dream or a vision get together and form a business, they create a shared vision and a shared passion that can energize a business and make it successful. The key word is shared. A vision not shared is a personal goal that may or may not support the business goals. Leo Hertzel has said that, "A goal is a dream with a deadline". Achieving our goals depends on being able to define, to live and to share our dreams. When a group shares a dream and works well together, they can generate an amazing amount of passion and energy in their work. What are you passionate about? What are your dreams about work and your business? Are you living them? Are your dreams compatible with your business vision? Are you bringing passion to what you do today? Are you committed to business or BSiness? ■

Discussion Questions:

1. What are you passionate about in your business? Is that where you spend the majority of your time? What dreams do you have for the business and your role in it? Are you living them?

2. Do you enjoy going to work every day? Do you look forward to it? Why? Why not?

Outrageous Managers follow their dreams and passions.

Valuing Differences

A Fortune 500 company continually selects clones of themselves to join their management team. They sink into groupthink, lose their creativity and continually lose market share.

An engineering firm only recruits from one school, the one the founder went to. They don't learn new approaches and become stagnant.

A management team continues to consist of all white middle class males. They experience very high turnover in the company, restrict their potential market and become very internally competitive.

We are all different. This is a good thing but we frequently treat differences as a disease and punish or exclude people who are different than we are. We start life with a worldview that everyone is the same as we are and that those who are different are wrong or sick. Nothing could be further from the truth. We are all perfect just as we are.

Many people and businesses have used the Myers-Briggs MBTI, True Colors, Keirsey Bates, Personalysis or some other instrument or program to find out about their preferences or personality type. These instruments and programs help lead to self awareness about our own preferences, personalities, biases and tendencies. More importantly, they help us to understand other personality types and how the differences are valuable and play equally important roles as our own. Knowledge and application of these differences can be invaluable in developing leadership, working (and personal) relationships, effective communication, teams and change efforts.

There are many other areas of difference that can lead to increased diversity and creativity or to conflict and disruption. We come from different ethnic backgrounds, genders, cultures, religions, age groups, social groups, educational backgrounds, work histories, sexual preferences, life histories, geographical areas and many other backgrounds that affect who we are and how we think, feel and act. Each of these areas contributes to our uniqueness and to how we contribute to our businesses and communities. We each bring different gifts and treasures and want to be valued for who we are. Tapping into and valuing those gifts and treasures is the opportunity and challenge of every manager.

Trusting and valuing differences doesn't come easily or naturally. Most of us were raised to distrust people different than ourselves and our families and we developed significant prejudices and biases. Rooting out and letting go of those fears and prejudices is a deep and difficult process but one that must be done and continue to be done. Intolerance or prejudice in business is not an option. Diversity is not only good business, it's the law.

Valuing and using our diversity leads to improved creativity, performance and customer relations, better working relationships, a more interesting workplace and a richer life. ■

Discussion Questions:

1. What prejudices or biases are present in your workplace?

2. How would your business improve with increased diversity? How will you do it?

Outrageous Managers thrive on differences.

Principled Negotiation

A manager negotiates salary with a candidate and gets the person for less than they are worth. The new hire leaves for a better paying job after they have just become productive.

A large company tightens their pricing because they sense that their vendors really need their business at this time. Their costs decrease but they can't get deliveries later when the market has changed and resources are scarce.

A procurement manager is afraid of conflict and continually pays too much for supplies.

Negotiation is the process of working toward agreement and getting what you want from others. Principled negotiation does that in such a way that it is a win-win outcome. Getting to a win-win outcome is not always easy. It requires that we stay rational, be prepared, allocate sufficient time, stay clear and quantitative in our objectives, maintain our working relationships and follow the rules for principled negotiation.

The toughest part of the process is to stay rational. Yes, we are all rational people and we think this should be easy. Actually, in stressful situations (negotiation can be very stressful) we rarely act in the way that we think we will. Extensive research and experience has shown that when situations get stressful, we act based on early emotional programming, rather than in a rational manner. This happens whenever:

- Voices get raised.

- We feel dominated or powerless.

- Issues get beyond our comprehension.

- The other people involved get emotional or abusive

- Our needs seem unattainable.

- External circumstances put pressure on us to win.

- We seek to dominate others.

- And in many other circumstances.

Constant attention is required to stay in a rational mode and keep bringing the negotiation back to a rational process. One of the reasons that negotiations frequently become irrational is that negotiations frequently involve the needs of one or more of the parties and needs are mostly emotional, subconscious or unconscious. Getting your needs met or helping the other party achieve their needs is very difficult when they can't be expressed clearly and rationally.

Another key element of the negotiation process is to define and maintain the working relationship. The purpose and importance of the relationship should be an integral part of the process. "Winning" the negotiation and losing a long term customer or supplier is not good business. Remember that relationships are difficult and that you are half the problem. To improve your relationships during negotiation: assume good intentions; solve negative conflict and promote positive conflict; work toward win-win solutions and pay attention to whether the outcome will help or hurt long term relations. A CEO of a high technology company put it best, "If you can negotiate a 10, settle for 8 and everyone will come out better".

The rules for principled negotiation are fairly easy and very helpful:

People. Separate the people from the problem

Interests. Focus on interests rather than positions

Options. Generate a variety of possibilities before deciding on the outcomes

Criteria. Insist that the result be based on some objective standard

So, negotiate rationally, pay attention to the relationship and follow the rules of principled negotiation. This will lead to better long term business performance and results. ■

Discussion Questions:

1. Are you too aggressive or competitive to achieve win-win solutions? Too timid?

2. How do you deal with emotion and stress? Are you sure?

Outrageous Managers create cooperation.

Conflict Sucks–
Or Does It?

*T*he head of a major division is brought in from outside the company. The heir apparent openly challenges everything the new division manger does and creates turmoil in the division for several years. The conflict ruins division performance and morale.

The two partners in a company originally complemented each other but grew further and further apart. The conflict divided the company and they eventually went out of business.

A diverse multi-cultural Board is put together to run a major training company. The group learns to value differences and accept widely divergent points of view. They thrive.

Conflicts are defined as apparent or real differences between people and are a daily occurrence in every business. Since conflicts arise from differences and all people are different, we need to learn to recognize, accept and deal with conflict. We can arbitrarily divide conflicts into two types: Positive conflicts that lead to learning and innovation; and Negative conflicts that lead to pain and divisiveness. It is important to distinguish which type is present and learn to adjust our behavior accordingly.

Most of us prefer to avoid conflict or to accommodate others when faced with differences. While these may occasionally be the appropriate responses because the issue is not important or we have no chance of other approaches, avoidance and accommodation normally lead to resentments, passive agreement or a lack of engagement. This behavior gives tremendous power over us to anyone willing to openly engage in conflict.

Positive conflicts are the honest disagreements and differing points of view that let us carefully look at policies, approaches and decisions from many points of view. Positive conflicts are where we truly celebrate differences and take advantage of the different backgrounds, talents, abilities and knowledge of all the participants in a business. Respecting people and their differences does not mean we have to agree with them. It means that we are willing to hear and respect their point of view and honestly and openly express our points of view. Through openly airing differences, we all learn and we become creative, growing businesses. Suppressing our opinions or those of others leads to groupthink and stagnation. Positive conflict needs to be encouraged.

Negative conflicts are those that personally attack others or attack the core values, vision, and mission of the company. They can be mean spirited or honest disagreements about the core premises the business is built on. Frequently the mean spirited conflicts are based on past history and resentments that have grown out of past differences. Processing honest disagreements about core values and visions can lead to the creation of a new shared vision and direction for the business or a decision to disagree and separate. Either outcome is preferable to a divided business that fails

Promote positive conflicts in the work place and solve the negative conflicts. Make sure you understand which type of conflict is happening and then use the appropriate models. ■

Discussion Questions:

1. Do you encourage others to disagree with you and express differing opinions? Why?

2. How do you deal with conflict? Do they get resolved? What is the effect?

Outrageous Managers love differences and positive conflict.

Models For Solving Negative Conflict

So, how do we deal with all these conflicts and get them resolved or at least minimized? Most conflicts are easily resolved using a very simple model:

1. Bring the individuals or groups in conflict together (with a facilitator).

2. Have both parties agree to try to honestly address the conflict(s).

3. Have each party express their view of the conflict and what they want.

4. Have each party paraphrase the other party's view and what they want.

5. Agree on similarities and points that are no longer in disagreement.

6. Define the differences and attempt to collaborate or compromise to reach a solution.

7. Follow up and ensure that the left over emotion doesn't undo the agreements.

A facilitator or mediator is frequently necessary to provide safety and ensure a fair discussion of the issues without personal attacks. The most difficult part of this process is to get the parties to express what they want. Remember that most of us want to avoid or accommodate during conflict so stating our needs is very risky. The facilitator needs to stay with this area until both parties have clearly expressed what they want. Paraphrasing the other person's needs and point of view is a key step that forces us to acknowledge that the other points of view exist. This normally resolves most issues—up until then we hope the disagreement will go away and we don't need to deal with it. Once it exists, we have to deal with it and we can move toward resolution. The above model will lead to resolution of all but the most stubborn and deep rooted of conflicts.

The very deep rooted and value based conflicts that are not resolved using this model can be addressed using the surrogate model. This model is based on the premise that we truly resist defining and dealing with our own conflicts and that the true nature of the conflict is usually common knowledge to everyone else in the business. Many businesses have developed rules for dealing with conflict that say we are obligated to go directly to the party we disagree with and resolve our own differences. A great theory that works very poorly in practice. What normally happens is that we seek out our closest friends or associates and discuss the issues with them instead of the party we disagree with. This is actually very natural behavior because it is safe and supportive.

The surrogate model builds on this natural behavior. The following steps are added at the beginning of the model discussed earlier:

1. Bring the individuals or groups in conflict together with their peers and a facilitator.

2. Have both parties agree to try to honestly address the conflict(s).

3. Have each party select a surrogate that they would like to support them in the process.

4. Have the surrogates express why they are willing to support their party in the process.

5. Have each surrogate express their view of the conflict and what they think is wanted.

6. Have each surrogate paraphrase the other party's view and what they want.

7. Have the surrogates discuss similarities and areas of agreement and difference.

8. Define the differences and attempt to collaborate or compromise to reach a solution.

9. Follow up and ensure that the left over emotion doesn't undo the agreements.

The surrogate's role really is to get the process started and get an honest description of the differences and conflict in the open as early as possible in the process. The primary parties are kept silent and listen in the first few steps, but experience has been that they quickly want to get involved and correct misstatements or misconceptions fairly early in the process. They then become actively engaged in resolving the issues. They may not enjoy the process but it does bring the issues out into the open and frequently results in very clear problem definitions and resolutions. As the primary parties take over the discussions, the surrogate role becomes a silent one of support.

Negative conflicts can normally be resolved and the resolving of those conflicts can have a positive effect on the business. Whether expressed or hidden, conflicts are a daily part of doing business. The expressed ones can have positive effects while the hidden or unexpressed ones always have negative effects. Business leaders need to be sensitive to the existence of negative conflicts and insist that they be dealt with as soon as possible. Negative conflicts affect everyone in a group–not just the primary people involved. ■

Discussion Questions:

1. Does conflict negatively affect your business? What will you do about it? When?

2. Are gossip and backbiting prevalent? Are you sure? How will you deal with it?

Outrageous Managers root out and resolve negative conflicts.

Coaching and Feedback

*T*he board of directors of a large national corporation is unhappy with the direction and performance of the CEO and the company. They feel that they are continually expressing this but no change happens. The CEO feels that he is not getting any clear direction. The CEO is eventually removed and the company suffers through another unnecessary change.

A manager continually gives his employees unsolicited feedback. They learn to fear and avoid the manager and performance declines.

A CEO consistently "coaches" his team through highlighting their shortcomings at team meetings. The management team meetings become unproductive and abusive.

We all need feedback and input from trusted associates to be effective as leaders, managers and business professionals. We also all seem to dislike hearing negative news or negative information about ourselves. The processes of giving and receiving feedback and providing and receiving coaching are very similar. They define safe and effective ways of learning about ourselves and our behavior in a way that we can hear the information and make necessary changes.

Coaching and feedback should not be confused with performance reviews or corrective actions by a manager. Performance reviews and corrective actions are very specific and direct. They define performance areas that need correction. Coaching and feedback are the learning processes that will help the individual learn how to change and improve their performance. Corrective action is used to stop something immediately and to point out problems. Feedback and coaching are used to develop new skills and abilities. Corrective action and performance reviews are initiated by the manager; feedback and coaching are initiated by the receiver.

The most important rule about giving and receiving feedback is that *feedback should never be given unless asked for*. There are many reasons for this crucial rule but the most important one seems to be that unless feedback is asked for, the receiver doesn't hear it and both the giver and receiver get frustrated. The other important factor in getting feedback from others is that *the receiver must ask specific questions.* The primary relationship that we set up to give and receive feedback in business is called coaching.

Coaching is the process of giving specific feedback (when asked for) to help business people achieve higher performance levels or develop specific skills and abilities. The business person contracts with a coach to gather data about their behavior in business situations and then to give the requested feedback. The contract defines the relationship, establishes very clear boundaries and allows for the development of trust between the coach and receiver. A critical boundary is that the person coached is always in charge and remains the decision maker on the content and duration of the process.

Coaches normally use an inquiry process to assist business people to learn and grow. Inquiry assumes that the business person already knows the material and needs help in accessing that knowledge and applying the knowledge in business situations. The inquiry process involves asking probing questions to help the business person to reflect on their behavior, explore other options, and make decisions for future actions. Inquiry can also be used to explore specific performance and accountability issues by reviewing previous commitments, defining the actions taken, discussing alternatives and defining specific action steps. Accountability for business performance is the critical process.

Coaching can be a high performance business tool. Coaching has a defined business purpose and results that can be easily measured. To get the most out of the process: clearly define the business purpose; define and develop the relationship with very clear boundaries; follow the process; act on the feedback; and continually measure the results and correct the contract as required. ∎

Discussion Questions:

1. Do you give feedback that is not requested? How will you change?

2. Who will you ask to coach you? On what subjects? Be specific!

Outrageous Managers model effective feedback and coaching.

You Are Invited...

A *large company brought in a new CEO to design and implement needed changes in the company. He worked with two executives to develop a plan and then told the managers and employees what they were to do. Nothing happened and no change took place. The CEO got frustrated and dictated more and more new policies. Nothing changed in over six months of effort. In traveling around the company to find out why change wasn't happening, the same answer was heard again and again. Why aren't you supporting the new direction and changes? I was never asked!!!*

Businesses are social as well as economic institutions. As social institutions, the same rules and stigmas apply that used to apply in high school where most of us learned our social behavior. Power was the ability to choose the players on a team or pick who would come to a party or lead an activity or event. Those of us who were selected felt empowered and "in". Those of us left out felt bad and resentful. Most of us have very clear memories of being invited to a key event or being chosen to play on a pick up team and the joy we felt. We also have clear memories of the shame of not being invited to something we wanted to attend or not being picked for the team.

Invitation was the key back then and it still is— especially in business. Invitation is an attitude and a way of doing business that works. Inviting managers and employees to join a team, attend a meeting, participate in a project, lead an event, make a presentation, support a vision and plan, comment on a new policy, etc. empowers them to make a choice and they feel included. Ordering someone to do the same thing may produce the stated action but will not produce the desired energy. Picture your own reaction and energy to the following pairs of statements:

You are invited to participate in building our vision and plan for the future. We have developed a vision that all of you will follow and implement.

The staff meeting is scheduled for 9:00 A.M. Monday, all staff will attend. You are invited to a discussion of key operating issues at 9:00 A.M. Monday.

Another company had two very similar divisions, each of them about $200 million in size and suffering from poor operating and financial performance. The leader of one of the divisions brought his people together and invited them to solve the issues and help design the changes necessary to turn the company around. They turned around within three months and all celebrated the difficult and successful changes. The other division leader continued his dictatorial approach and lost the company over a hundred million dollars.

You are invited to look at how you lead your company, function or workspace. Do you include rather than exclude? Do you invite rather than demand? Do you listen rather than tell? Do you create positive energy or produce stigma and shame? It's your choice. ■

Discussion Questions:

1. Who are you excluding from your team? Why? What action will you take?

2. How can you get more of your company involved in making your plans work? What specific steps will you take? Write out the invitation.

Outrageous Managers include and invite.

Chapter 4
Mastering The Truth

Mastering a subject is defined as developing excellent skill and proficiency in that area. Mastering the truth in organizations and business is an ongoing process of learning about and applying the truth. Truth is defined as the actuality or reality of a situation. All business decisions and actions assume that we are dealing with the truth of a situation. We have all been told to tell the truth from our earliest years and most of us try our best to be truthful. Yet the truth is elusive, especially in organizations. In a survey of 40,000 Americans, 93% admitted to lying regularly at work (Fast Company Magazine). This is not a problem–it's an epidemic and it's not acceptable. Managing our organizations and businesses requires that we know the truth and base our decisions on actuality and reality.

Models of Truth

Mastering the truth has many levels and dimensions. In this chapter we will explore four levels or dimensions of truth. The survey above only looked at the first and second dimension of truth–the factual and outer dimensions of truth. Those are the easiest dimensions and yet we don't do them well. The third and fourth dimensions of truth are more elusive. Individual truth is also easier than arriving at the truth for groups or organizations. Group dynamics and norms make it more difficult for groups or teams to get to the truth of situations. Organization cultures and systems either support discovering the truth or make it next to impossible.

This chapter will explore some basic principles and how they apply to organizations and business. Let's start with some basic ideas:

- Truth is a quest because it takes effort and commitment to discover the truth.

- Truth is an internal process because we frequently need to go inside ourselves to discover what we believe about a situation and our own truth about a situation.

- Truth is also an external process because discovering the truth of a situation normally requires interaction with others.

- The truth of a situation isn't always obvious. It takes attention and some effort to discover the truth.

- Truth is based on trusting ourselves and our opinions and beliefs–when we don't trust ourselves we hold back and don't express what we think and feel.

- Truth is based on trusting others. When we don't trust others we don't solicit their input and get to the truth of situations.

- Trust is based on others trusting us, especially when we are in positions of authority. If people don't trust us they will not openly express the truth.

- Truth takes courage. Both the quest to find the truth and the willingness to express it take an enormous amount of courage.

- Truth is an ongoing inquiry. What was true in the past may or may not continue to be true today or in the future as new knowledge and data become available.

- Fear blocks us from access to the truth. Our own truth and the truth of other people.

- Truth is very personal. We have strong opinions about what is true and usually strong feelings about those opinions.

- Truth is frequently intuitive. We frequently know intuitively when something feels right or does not feel right and our bodies react when we feel those intuitions.

The truth of a situation is thus significantly affected by two interrelated factors:

1. The ability to understand and discover the actual truth of the situation. This quest for understanding and discovery has given birth to the information age and the proliferation of data and information generated daily. This ability is also very affected by the models we use and the levels of truth that apply to the situation.

2. The trust to speak the truth. Establishing trust and creating environments where people are free to speak the truth has given birth to the development of leadership, teams and the whole area of human resource development.

The Types and Levels of Truth

The quest for understanding and discovery gets more interesting as we explore the truth at deeper levels and add dimensions. Trust gets more involved as we move from individuals looking for the truth to groups and organizations. The levels of truth are summarized in the following table.

Levels of Truth

Levels	Factors	Pattern	Examples
I Sensation	Facts, Raw	Raw Data Thoughts and Feelings	A Line
II Rational/ Duality	Identification of Thoughts and	Euclidean Geometry	A Surface A Circle The World is Flat
III Intellect (Mind and Emotion)	Systems, Frameworks Images, Metaphors	Science, Medicine Physics, Philosophy Senge, Freud	A Sphere The World is Round
IV Mythology/ Mysticism	Self-Organizing Systems	Quantum Physics Einstein, Capra Wheatley, Jung Joseph Campbell	The Universe Space—Time
V Unity			

We could also look at the interaction of the levels of truth and the complexity of moving from individuals to organizations. That matrix is shown below.

Levels And Types Of Truth

Levels/ Types	Individual	Group	Organization
I Factual	Sensations	Facts	Data
II Rational	Thoughts and Feelings Performance	Consensus Procedures	Patterns Practices
III Systemic	Mental and Emotional Intelligence Frameworks	Values and Processes Images	Operating Principles Systems
IV Mythic	Archetypes and Intuitions Unconscious	Group Integration Group Unconscious	Self-Organizing Systems Organization Unconscious

Level I Truth

The first level of truth looks at the raw sensations, facts and data, with no processing function. The first level is true by definition, it is what we see, hear, smell, etc. As we accumulate impulses and inputs, we develop facts and then data. Joe Friday in Dragnet was the exemplar of this level. He was famous for interviewing people and insisting on "just the facts". For Joe, the facts were the story and all that was necessary.

Level II Truth

The second level of truth is where the interpretation begins and we move from the raw data to perceptions, thoughts and feelings about the data. Data are organized into two dimensional lists and patterns. We have awareness of the data and can decide whether to share it, alter it or report it. There is a duality involved that helps us decide whether it is true or false, right or wrong, safe or unsafe, important or unimportant, etc. All rule based organizations operate at this second level. Rules, procedures and practices are developed for an organization and then they are followed or not followed. The creators of the rules may work at a deeper level of truth but they expect people to follow their rules and procedures. Decisions are linear and simple.

Most organizations and all bureaucracies operate at this second level of truth. Bureaucratic organizations were based on the work of Max Weber and were set up to depersonalize work and ensure the separation of work from the home because the interference of family or emotion in the rationalization of work would be counterproductive. Weber assumed that managers would be highly principled and would not abuse or misuse the total power and control that this organizational form provided. Many writers have defined this organizational form as a "machine" bureaucracy because people are treated as machines and not expected to think or feel. It is a powerful image.

The second level is the level of truth where 93% of those surveyed reported that they regularly lie. Since this level is dualistic, people are in compliance with the rules or they are not. If they are not, there are consequences and these consequences are threatening to the person. People operating in these bureaucracies are put into a bind. If they tell the truth about negative information, they face personal negative consequences. Weber assumed that all people will tell the truth but a century of this form of organization has proven that this is not the case. Does this mean that people are unable to tell the truth? Not at all! But it raises many questions about how we get to the truth and how to encourage and support people telling the truth.

One study of the phenomena of what happens in bureaucracy, *Crimes of Obedience* by Kelman and Hamilton, observed that social influence is a major factor affecting whether people adhere to the rules and roles of society and tell the truth. The social rules are frequently not the organization rules but those of the informal social group to which the person belongs. The need to conform to the social group can be much stronger than the need to report accurately to the organization.

When the goals and practices of the social group are different than the organization goals, the person will normally follow the social norms instead of the organization rules and guidelines. In almost all bureaucracies, the social roles are anti-organizational and work against the power and control of the bureaucracy. This is understandable when we acknowledge that the bureaucracy is by definition impersonal and social roles are personal. People have strong personal needs for affiliation and belonging and normally conform to social norms.

Peter Block, in his book *The Empowered Manager*, describes the bureaucratic process as the process of dependency. A bureaucracy makes people dependent on their supervisors for their continued employment, raises, promotions, rewards, punishments and other factors. This dependency takes away their initiative and independence and replaces them with compliance and appeasement. This leads to telling our supervisors what they want to hear rather than all the details of what is happening. The informal social groups support this behavior of withholding information and appeasing the supervisor.

The bottom line is that organizations operating at the second level of truth rarely develop trust and thus rarely operate based on the truth. The rule based organization is not very complex and it does not have the personal and social components that lead to developing trust. Those components are developed at the third level.

Level III Truth

The third level of truth is the world of systems, science, medicine and philosophy. It is also the world of mental intelligence and emotional intelligence. Answers are far more complex at the third level and require looking beyond the facts and the easy rational answers to find what is really happening in the situation. Dualism is out and ambiguity and broader three dimensional thinking is in.

Bolman and Deal describe management at this stage as happening in frameworks. To discover the truth of situations we need to see whether the situation fits into the rational/structural frame, the human resource frame, the political frame or the cultural/symbolic frame. Analyzing the situation from all four perspectives helps to bring us closer to the truth. Gareth Morgan uses metaphors and images to apply the same approach. His *Images of Organizations* implies that we need to understand the underlying principles or metaphors that describe the situation to discover the truth. His images include organizations as machines, organisms, brains, cultures, political systems, psychic prisons and instruments of domination.

These are powerful images that help us to understand the reality or actuality of what is happening in a situation, i.e., the truth. Both of these sources are saying that we must look beyond the outer appearances of what is happening to find the broader causes and reasons. This is the systems approach. Any or all of the frames and images may be operating in a situation and we need to understand which are operating and how they interact to understand the system.

Social Truth

The third dimension of truth also begins to bring the whole person to work. Applying intelligence to situations includes looking not only at the mental models, philosophies and systems, but also at the emotional intelligence and processes that begin to build trust and allow the truth to be spoken. Daniel Goleman's book, *Emotional Intelligence*, defines five major abilities of emotional intelligence:

1. Knowing one's emotions. Developing the self awareness of what one is feeling in the moment and the continuing ability to monitor feelings as they occur.

2. Managing emotions. The ability to react and respond appropriately in situations and to bounce back from negative or harmful situations.

3. Motivating oneself. The ability to delay gratification and marshal emotions in the pursuit of a goal.

4. Recognizing emotions in others. The ability to empathize with others and the ability to socially analyze situations to determine what others are feeling.

5. Handling relationships. The ability to develop excellent relationships and deal with the emotions of others. (See the chapter on energizing relationships)

Those with high emotional intelligence have mastered the emotional world to the extent that they have developed excellent social skills. They can organize groups, negotiate solutions, relate personally with others and know what is happening socially in situations.

There are two aspects of this emotional intelligence that directly affect our pursuit of the truth: The social truth of the situation; and the effect of the social factors on trust.

The social truth of a situation is a new concept and one whose time has come. We have all walked into situations where we immediately knew we were comfortable and fit in. We felt good being there and were totally present to participate in whatever was happening. We have also walked into situations where we were immediately uncomfortable and knew that we wanted to leave. There are also a whole gamut of situations in between those two situations where we were partially comfortable or partially uncomfortable.

While comfort may not have been our primary concern, these situations can start to give us a picture of the social truth about a situation. The social truth of a situation includes such factors as safety, comfort, diversity, energy, familiarity, interest and many others. Maslow's hierarchy of needs have been used for some time and yet they have never been translated into social truth because organizations have remained far too rational and resistant to human factors. As

Maslow stated, the basic needs must be met or they dominate our consciousness and restrict us from doing our work.

Assuming that the basic physiological needs have been met, the social needs that need to be met are safety (especially protection from emotional harm), affection, belonging, acceptance, friendship, autonomy, status, recognition and attention. Without arguing what should or should not be part of such a list, there are social factors that significantly affect our working life. Our emotional assessment of these factors defines our social truth. Our social truth thus defines whether or not situations, groups, organizations or working relationships are or are not emotionally working for us.

A good hostess is very socially adept and instinctively knows how to organize functions and how to ensure that everyone who attends will enjoy themselves and have a good experience. A good manager or leader must become equally socially adept and learn how to provide organizations and processes that meet the social needs of their people. The good manager must know instinctively whether the social truth of the situation is positive and supporting the organization goals or negative and working against the organization goals. The manager must have high emotional intelligence and use it to continually perform social analyses of their business situations. They also need to use that emotional intelligence to resolve social issues that arise and re-energize the social structures and working relationships.

Trust is measured by the social truth of the situation. Without trust, people are not free to tell the truth. Our emotions tell us whether or not to trust someone. We have feelings and instincts about people we work with and work for. When actions take place that betray our trust, we instinctively withdraw emotionally and begin to sever the trust and the commitment to support that person and their goals. When a group does not trust their leader or manager, then that group can no longer be effectively led by that person.

Trust has both rational and emotional components. If we act in congruence with our stated principles and values, then people start to trust our actions. When we start to support the growth and meet the social needs of people we work with, then we start to develop emotional trust. When we attack other people or threaten their emotional safety, we start to lose their emotional trust and the working relationship suffers. I may respect someone who acts congruently but I don't trust them until I feel right about my working relationship with them.

More people leave organizations because of failed working relationships than for any other reason. Most working relationships fail because of the social truth of the situation and the emotional factors involved. Analyzing the social truth in our organizations is as important as the other types of truth. The social truth is actually more important because we don't hear the rational truth if we haven't developed trust by paying attention to the social truth.

Level IV Truth

Truth at level four is where rational and emotional intelligence integrate, where systems become self-organizing, where time integrates with space and where we delve into the collective unconscious. It is the realm of quantum physics, transpersonal psychology, quantum healing, spirit, art, mythology, transformative leadership, intuition, creativity and energy. Luckily, we don't have to learn quantum physics and transpersonal psychology to develop level four truth. Actually, the opposite is true, developing level four truth is necessary to understand quantum physics and transpersonal psychology. While truth at level three was based on probability and analysis, level four truth begins the process of direct apprehension, insight, intuition and knowing. It is where our minds interact with our imaginations.

Level four truth is not intellectual or difficult. Everyone has direct access to this level of truth and can use it any time they choose. Actually, we were all born with abilities at this level and used them frequently in childhood. Daydreaming, fantasy and creative play come from this level and were natural abilities we all used. In school, we were taught to leave these abilities behind and to become scientific and rational. It is now time to reclaim those abilities and use them. We need our imaginations to be creative and to have fun.

Level three truth was based on learning. Peter Senge summarized level three as becoming learning organizations. Level four truth is based on unlearning. It is where we leave structured thought, critical thinking and analysis behind. We unclutter our minds and let them roam free. The results are startling and amazing. Business groups that are invited to go on a journey to the future through simple relaxation and guided imagery always discover new things about themselves and their organizations. Through their imaginations, they can see pictures of the future and get clarity on their businesses that they can't get at other levels.

The fastest growing cultural segment in the United States has been called the Integral Culture by sociologist Paul Ray. Based on a study sponsored by the Fetzer Foundation, this Integral Culture of "Cultural Creatives" consists of 44 million adults in the U.S. who are active believers in and users of level four truth. Most of these cultural creatives are fairly affluent and educated, which means that they are business or organizational managers, leaders and professionals. While business and education still have a strong rational bias, the majority of the managers and leaders of those organizations and businesses do not. Many recent studies of leaders have shown that successful leaders have well developed intuitive skills and are highly creative. Visioning, a leadership requisite, requires level four intuitive abilities.

Albert Einstein is often quoted as saying that imagination is more important than knowledge. That statement starts to help define the differences between level three and level four truth. Some of those differences are summarized in the following table.

Level III Truth	Level IV Truth
Sphere	Universe
Science	Art
Left Brain	Right Brain/Whole Brain
Intelligence	Imagination
Thinking and Feeling	Intuition
Analysis	Knowing
Structured	Self-Organized
Planning	Visioning
Managing	Leading
Operating	Creating
Work	Flow
Masculine and Feminine	Integrated
Objective	Passionate
Learning	Unlearning
Stressed	Relaxed
Focus	Energy
Process	Synergy
Mind and Heart	Soul

Einstein is also often quoted as saying that no problem can be solved from the level of consciousness that created it. We could equate our levels of truth to levels of consciousness and say that second level problems must be solved at the third level, and third level problems must be solved at the fourth level. Certainly any type of transition would require third level truth and consciousness, and any transformation requires fourth level truth and consciousness.

The third level of truth is like an orchestra with everyone on the same page and following the baton of the conductor. The fourth level of truth is like jazz, with everyone playing the same song or piece and creating variations and embellishments as they play. The movie *Amadeus* was wonderfully instructive. Salieri kept trying to create new music from the third dimension and his music was very structured but never flowed and was frankly boring and uninspired. Mozart effortlessly created beautiful music from his imagination and intuition. They operated at different levels of consciousness.

The third dimension of truth worked well in the industrial age, but the industrial age is over. Businesses and organizations now need to develop their abilities to operate at the fourth level. Leadership, creativity, passion, energy and synergy are no longer optional. These are required for the business and organization that will succeed in the new millenium. Businesses and business people need to develop and have soul. The music metaphors may be helpful again. Salieri's music had no soul. Mozart's music has wonderful soul. Regardless of the type of music, we can tell when it has soul and when it doesn't. We can also listen to a soloist or group and intuitively know whether they put soul into their music. The truth is that we can also walk into a business and immediately know whether they put soul into what they do. If they do, it is an exiting place that is alive with positive energy. If they don't, it is flat and dead.

Fritjof Capra, in his book *The Turning Point*, describes the shift from the third dimension to the fourth dimension in the chapter titled "The Systems View of Life". The key element in the transformation or evolution from the third dimension to the fourth dimension is the development of consciousness and the process of becoming alive. In the third dimension, we are emerging according to someone else's plan. Life is determined by preset structures and we seek to find out what they are but can't change or influence the preset structures. In the fourth dimension, we become alive, define our own structures and create our own universe. Margaret Wheatley talks about the same phenomena in her book *Leadership and The New Science.* Organizations who want to survive in the next millenium will have to be alive. They will have to create themselves again and again and become highly creative.

The emerging literature on intuition and creativity in organizations confirms that organizations need to shift to the fourth level of truth and to become conscious and alive. The good news is that it can be done and that it can be fun. Individually, it is the process of developing your intuition and learning to trust it. Develop your own approaches to connecting to your inner wisdom and your connection to your creative soul. Become outrageous and creative. Jack Hawley calls this *Reawakening The Spirit in Work.* His book describes several journeys that we might take to develop these abilities and gives an excellent bibliography. Choose the processes that work for you. There is no right way to do this, there are many ways and the right ones are those you connect with and that work for you.

At the group level it is the process of developing group energy and starting to develop a group consciousness. Group consciousness means a new level of awareness at the group level, a level where the group is conscious of its own processes and develops group intuition or insight. Another way to say this is that the group can tap into their collective unconscious. Groups need to openly talk about their intuition and creativity. Try unusual processes and work together to develop group intuition. When discussing these topics with groups, it is always amazing how many people have wanted to do this for a long time but felt they couldn't because these topics are not appropriate for business. Intuitives and fourth dimension creatives are a significant part of the population but still remain in the closet. It is time to come out of the closet and start getting your groups to work at the fourth dimension.

At the organization level, it is a major process of developing, modeling, encouraging and using fourth dimension truth throughout the organization. It is the process of transforming the leadership of the organization and then the organization itself. This is a long term process. Start small with yourself and then your management team. The spread through the organization will then be more organic than linear. As the process begins, you will be surprised at both the support that will come from unexpected places and the resistance that will be vocal and very strong. ∎

The Five Myths of Business Ethics

A *steel mill in Alabama spews toxic smoke into the atmosphere and pollutes the air and lungs of the local population. They pay the minimal fine and call it a business decision.*

Hundreds of engineers, government regulators, project managers and business managers participate in a scheme to defraud the North Slope Borough in Alaska of hundreds of millions of dollars. They individually claim that they all made ethical business decisions.

Business ethics is a difficult and controversial subject. We all think we are ethical and respond strongly to the unethical acts of others. Yet business in general is **not** perceived as being ethical. How can this be? How can we be individually ethical and collectively unethical? The answer may lie in looking at five myths about business ethics.

Myth #1: *Having a code of ethics leads to ethical decisions and actions.* Research has shown again and again that companies with codes of ethics are equally likely to make unethical decisions and foster unethical actions as those with no written code of ethics.

Myth #2: *Business decisions are conscious.* Most studies of executives show that the decision process is rarely separated from the action. Decisions are made on the fly and in the heat of the moment. Having the time to think and mull over issues is a myth.

Myth #3: *Business decisions are logical.* Clear thinking and logical decision making are prized by executives. Yet in difficult and stressful situations, over 90% of managers make decisions based on early socialized decision rules and are not aware they do that.

Myth #4: *Ethics are relative.* The most common business belief about ethics is that they are based on individual religious and/or moral beliefs and principles and thus should be relative and left up to the individual. Extensive research shows that there are universal principles that govern all religious and moral beliefs and that can be universally applied.

Myth #5: *We make our own decisions.* Social psychologists have shown that most of us will go along with decisions that make no sense to get along with our peers and feel like we belong. Group think and group pressure normally affect our decisions.

These myths lead to the conclusion that we do not actively make unethical decisions, *we normally do not consider the ethics of the decision or action at all.* The key to ethical decision making and ethical business actions is to force yourself and your business associates to consciously consider the ethical implications of decisions and actions. Including ethical reviews of decisions and actions in regularly scheduled meetings can help to overcome the five myths of business ethics and improve your business decisions. Another interesting myth is that business results are negatively affected by business ethics. Most companies have found that business ethics and excellent results are synonymous. ■

Discussion Questions:

1. Which ethical myths are prevalent in your organization? How will you kill them?

2. What are the values or principles that you want to drive your decisions? How will you ensure that they are known and used? What specific steps will you take?

Outrageous Managers abhor unethical behavior.

The Roles We Play

*T*he ringleaders of a scheme to defraud the Native
Alaskan people of several hundred million dollars in
the North Slope Borough of Alaska were convicted in
federal court and sent to prison. There was a supporting cast of
about two hundred engineers, project managers, government
agency managers, accountants, bureaucrats and others who were
charged with making sure that the scheme to defraud never happened. When asked how something this large and obvious could
go on for so long and how they could participate in it, they
almost all replied that they were only doing their job. If the companies were making excess money, that was only good business.
This was not in the old West in the late 1800s, it was in the
United States in 1990.

In essence, the people interviewed were saying
that they were playing their role. Many of them knew
on some level that what they were doing was wrong
and several of them were becoming physically ill
because of their involvement. Yet, they were more
compelled to continue playing their role than calling a
halt to the scheme–to the wholesale theft of hundreds
of millions of dollars. These were not arch criminals
masterminding a heist, they were business men playing a defined role.

While playing our roles, we can sabotage our
companies, steal, start internal political wars, encourage poor performance or slowdowns, cheat on our
budgets, lie about what happened in situations, hide

bad news, bribe foreign governments or domestic suppliers, falsify records, exaggerate expense accounts, drink on the job, and do many other things that we would not normally expect from professional and managerial people.

Social psychologists define roles as the functions people perform when they are in a specific position and social context. The roles we play significantly influence our beliefs and attitudes while in that role and also define the limits of appropriate or acceptable behavior. The socialized expectations of the role and the reference group normally determine behavior in that context much more than our individual beliefs, attitudes or values. We are socialized into work roles by those who hire us and by the group we work with. Success on the job is normally associated with fitting in and adopting the company's beliefs, attitudes and values while on the job.

The power of the role over an individual's behavior will vary depending on the individual's conscious commitment to their own beliefs, attitudes and values. In some cases, the forces to comply with group norms and to stay within defined role expectations are very compelling. The North Slope Borough scheme appears to be one of those cases.

Business leaders and managers are responsible for the behavior and actions of their people. We can strongly influence that behavior by defining and establishing business roles that express our vision for the business and that will be consistent with our beliefs and values. Operating based on a commitment to the truth can help define positive business roles. ■

Discussion Questions:

1. What values drive behavior in your organization? Are they consistent with your personal values?

2. What level of truth is prevalent in your business? What would you like it to be?

Outrageous Managers instill positive business values.

Politically Direct

*T*he owner of a consulting firm is frustrated. A new sales director is working very hard, but results are less than optimal. The owner refuses to address the performance issue directly for fear this employee will leave the company. Instead, the owner is now planning all sales and marketing activities and giving specific assignments to the sales director. The sales director feels like he is being micro-managed, yet doesn't understand why.

The owners of a distribution company do not want to share the company's financial statements with their key managers because this year's results are running less than budget. They fear that the unsatisfactory performance will de-motivate their staff.

A controller in another business is stressed out. The company's financial statements are behind three months, and invoices may be two to three weeks late, but neither the owner nor the operations manager know for sure. Profitability and cash flow are beginning to become precarious. The principals do not want to address this issue for fear the stressed controller will snap and leave the practice.

A young CEO in a turn-around situation halts a planning and budgeting process shortly after starting it. She wants her management team to focus on current problem solving. The management team is frustrated because the root causes of the current problems are never completely dealt with and they keep reoccurring.

There has been a tendency for some time to be politically correct. Politically correct means a problem gets a new name so that it doesn't have to be dealt with head-on or maybe it doesn't get dealt with it at all. We see this in our local, state and national government everyday and our taxes reflect it. Failing to deal with government problems head-on results in major waste and super budget overruns. Failing to deal with them in business can lead to law suits and bankruptcy.

Politically correct businesses may spend significant time managing unmet sales, profit and quality goals. They may also spend a lot of time with employee morale and customer service issues. Businesses managed using the politically correct model typically have serious financial, operating and performance issues.

Politically correct communication comes from fear of telling the truth, operating at the second level of truth and trying to take care of other people's feelings. It doesn't work. Politically direct communication comes from courage, operating at the third or fourth level of truth and a commitment to discovering and speaking the truth. It not only works, it leads to better performance and improved business results. ■

Discussion Questions:

1. Do you always speak the truth about your business and your performance?

2. Do you demand that your managers, suppliers and salespeople also speak the truth?

Outrageous Managers are very direct and speak the truth.

Business
Metaphors

Systems thinking is the ability to see the whole picture of our business as an integrated, cohesive entity that is interdependent and alive. Yes, alive. When we create or grow a business, we start something that takes on a life of its own. It develops in expected and totally unexpected ways. Just as our own life takes many twists and turns, the life of a business is a journey that can't be controlled or anticipated. We can aim it from time to time and we can enjoy the ride. We can also learn to appreciate the complexities, apparent contradictions, challenges, inspirations, serendipitous happenings, coincidences and chaotic events that are part of the journey.

The easiest way for me to see and understand systems is to use metaphors. In the early and even late industrial age, businesses used the machine metaphor to understand their systems. The goal was high output manufacturing where we wanted all the products to be the same. People were there to serve and act like the machines which were the expensive part of the business and produced the output. Machines lasted a long time and only needed people to feed them, oil them and distribute the output. The ultimate business acted like "a well oiled machine". How many of your businesses look like that today? What machines do you use? How long have you had them? Most of us use computers and change them fairly frequently. But that's another metaphor.

The information age seems to have adopted the computer as the metaphor to understand systems. Computers process tons of data and people are there to input, analyze and distribute data. The goal is to downsize, outsource, use robotics or replace people with machines or temporary people who are young. Bright information processors can make the computers do even more. So, people are really seen as another type of machine, but one that doesn't last very long and needs to be replaced often. Not very comforting.

Another metaphor that is used fairly often is to view businesses as organic systems. Organic systems (like trees) require planting, fertilizer or nourishment, some nurturing, sun and water. These systems then grow according to preprogrammed genetic patterns. They are alive in that they are organic but really only grow and flourish in predictable ways. This metaphor fits people better but puts them in boxes and views them as unable to have original thoughts or act in creative ways. How many of our businesses will survive and flourish today if we only follow predictable patterns and can't adapt and change. Some businesses actually operate this way and do very well. The majority of us are in a world that requires constant change and creativity, the world of chaos or permanent white water.

The metaphor that I find to work for most businesses is to view them as living, creative interdependent systems. Businesses are like people. They are born, go through infancy and early growth, suffer through the teen age years and adolescence, mature, have relationships with others, get injured or hurt, adapt, move and if not cared for–die. Businesses are unpredictable in many ways, enjoyable in others, can have wonderful growth spurts, can decline and can adapt, change and create new ways of operating. With this metaphor, we can see that businesses have a physical body, a mind, a heart and a soul.

The machine metaphors only recognize the physical body of the business and the computer metaphor only sees the body and the programmed mind. The computer metaphor also ensures that our businesses never grow up by continually turning over those who start to mature. In the worst case, this is like creating the lost boys of Peter Pan or worse, a business that is always adolescent. Imagine a business that is perpetually staffed by teenagers who never get to grow out of that phase. The human metaphor acknowledges that the business is alive and able to think and feel on its own. A corporation is defined as a separate entity by law and the human systems metaphor gives this separate entity life.

If our businesses are alive and have human qualities, then they need to be cared for in ways similar to caring for humans. They need nurturing and feeding while they are young, they need room to create and grow during childhood, they need to mature and separate from their parents during adolescence, and they need to grow in wisdom and mature during mid life. They need attention to their physical well being–proper foods, exercise, attention to health and well being. They need mental development through training in the basics of the business and ongoing learning programs. They need attention to the relationships within the business and with others in their market-place and community. They also need to provide some shared values and higher purpose or meaning for their members. Healthy humans are very productive and creative and enjoy working and accomplishing goals. Healthy businesses are no different. ∎

Discussion Questions:

1. What metaphor is inherently driving your company? Does it work? Is it alive?

2. What metaphor would you like to drive your company? How will you give it life?

Outrageous Managers nurture creativity and growth.

Business
Intuition

A company goes through an extensive hiring process and picks a new manager who doesn't work out. The hiring group later comments that they knew that it wouldn't.

A bold entrepreneur starts a new business that everyone says will fail and becomes remarkably successful. He credits his success to following his dream and a hunch.

Business wisdom used to be equated with rational decision processes and detailed analysis. The worst thing someone could become known as was a hip shooter, a gut follower, a loose cannon or a hunch player. Business was serious and scientific. It still is and yet that doesn't always get the job done. Rational processes work in certain situations and can be the right tool when we have the data and time, and the situation lends itself to analysis. But what about those sticky situations where the situation is not black and white, but mostly gray. We don't have the time, the data or the ability to use analytical processes. What about questions about people, relationships, strategy, culture, politics, ethics, leadership, innovation, and the many other areas of business that can't be analyzed to find the right answer? How do we make those decisions? As we take on more and more responsibility in business, we rely more on experience and intuition.

Intuition is the knowing or learning of something without the conscious use of reason. Intuition is the gathering of information from an inner source or sixth sense as opposed to the five primary senses of sight, sound, touch, smell and taste. Business leaders use intuition constantly in their dealings with customers, suppliers, employees, decisions and problems. In most cases our decisions are instantaneous and without conscious thought–in other words they are intuitive decisions. Do I want to do business with this person? How should I approach this customer? Are things going well? What would be the right group to handle this problem? Is my executive team functioning well? These are all questions we answer intuitively (and sometimes rationally) every day.

Most of us check our intuition only after the decisions have been made. We use our intuition passively as a check on ourselves by seeing how we feel about the decision. We can get a queasy feeling in our gut, or a sense that we made a mistake, or an energy burst, or a sudden insight. The intuition can be mental, emotional, physical or even spiritual. What we do with these intuitions depends on how much we have developed our intuitive abilities and how much we have learned to trust them. It also depends on the business culture and whether intuitive decisions are accepted and encouraged or seen as dangerous and unprofessional. Many businesses still have a strong bias toward rational decisions.

Making proactive intuitive decisions is an ability that all of us can learn and develop.

1. Quiet the mind. Relaxation, exercise, walking, meditation or other methods can help.

2. Learn to focus your attention on your intuitive source. Don't focus on the problem.

3. Allow intuitions to come without judgment or interference. Accept what comes. Develop and

use your intuition to make better decisions in all the gray areas of business. ■

Discussion Questions:

1. Do you encourage or stifle the use of intuition in your business? How?

2. Who in your company brings the intuitive insights that challenge your traditional thinking? Are those insights valued and rewarded?

Outrageous Managers value and use their intuition.

Gender As A
Business Issue

Relations between men and women are a business issue as well as a highly charged social issue. To date, changes have come about through laws and rules about social behavior at work. While these laws and rules are necessary to reach the goal of changed behavior, behavior is not a rational or legal issue.

Most behavioral models describe behavior as the resulting action of personal beliefs, attitudes and values within the context of a specific situation. Changes in behavior patterns around gender issues involve beliefs about caring, protection, competition, power, fairness, equality, relationships, masculinity, femininity, attraction, success, and many other emotionally charged issues. The changes in the workplace reflect significant changes in defining the masculine and feminine gender ideals–or what society now believes men and women should be and how they should behave at work. This gender ideal is different than the gender role–or what is defined as the actual behaviors, beliefs, attitudes and conditions of a specific group of men and women at work.

Masculine and feminine stereotypes around behavior are inaccurate and damaging in looking at gender issues at work. There are also no agreed upon definitions of masculinity or femininity, or what factors cause or mold them. There is some agreement that gender roles are changing but there is no agreement on the gender ideal or what the new roles should or will be. The gender role of many present business managers and leaders was defined during their upbringing in the 1940s, 1950s and 1960s and their indoctrination into the workplace in the 1960s and 1970s.

Changing gender roles at work is not a simple process. It involves inner work to examine the sources of beliefs, values and attitudes and deep processes to replace them with new ones that might be closer to the new ideal. This is a transformational rather than a simple change process. The transformational process to change existing gender roles involves the need to express the beliefs and attitudes that are changing and the feelings around them. It is not presently safe to do that in the workplace. Expressing those beliefs and attitudes would be career threatening, so most of the emotion, confusion and frustration surrounding the changes at work stay bottled up, preventing the desired changes. The transformation process is equally dangerous and difficult for men and women. Both groups are changing and neither is safe to express who they are at work.

Transforming the gender roles at work will be successful only if both men and women and the relationships between them are healed. There has been little done to deal with the changes of men's and women's roles at work and to help define the new identity and social reality at work. The social truth of gender issues is being ignored. There has also been very little work done to help men and women through these major changes to bring about the healing of the system. Gender roles are being rewritten and changed by business. The chapters on change and working relationships help define some steps that will help organizations move through this major transformation. ■

Discussion Questions:

1. Is it safe to express frustration and anger over gender role changes where you work? Where can you express those feelings?

2. What is your process for dealing with gender role changes in your business? Who is leading the transformation?

Outrageous Managers embrace the social truth of gender issues at work.

Men's Changing Roles At Work

*T*he CFO of a major corporation has spent twenty years learning the patriarchal way of managing the financial aspects of the corporation and how to take care of the women who work for him. He's confused when he is now seen as outdated and is put out to pasture.

When I was growing up and entering the workforce, men were the providers for the family and expected to work, compete, get ahead and succeed. Women raised the families and took care of the home. This was not that long ago. Roles and expectations were clear. I can remember clearly when I was first confronted by a feminist at work. A female attorney took great exception to my language while I was helping to reorganize a law firm. At the time I didn't know what the big deal was and was taken aback by her behavior. I felt wronged and attacked.

Over time, my understanding and my behavior have changed. It hasn't been easy and it certainly wasn't a clearly defined path that could be learned through reading a book or going through a training program. The changes required were much deeper than that. All my upbringing, education, early work experiences and mentors had taught me a way of being at work that was no longer applicable or acceptable. There were no new mentors to lead the way to the new ways of being at work. Men really were under attack and eventually were on the defensive. Men were seen as dominant at work and the oppressor and women (and minorities) were the victims. This was not a change, it was a revolution.

There are many workshops on gender issues in the workplace today and they are all about the new roles of women. New laws and human resource policies define discrimination in the work place and the penalties for non-compliance. These are positive developments and are significantly changing our businesses–as well as creating confusion for men at work. How do we define masculinity in the workplace today? What is expected of us as men? Who are our models? Where do we learn about our new masculine work roles?

I don't claim to have the answers to this issue–it is far too complex. I do have some suggestions for processes that may lead to solutions.

1. Acknowledge that the changing masculine gender role is an important business problem and needs to be dealt with in the workplace.

2. Provide a safe place for men to openly discuss and dialog on these issues and to express their feelings and explore their beliefs and attitudes.

3. Form men's groups in the workplace to provide ongoing education, support and assistance to men going through these transformational changes.

4. Find men who have successfully gone through this transformation to mentor other men going through the process and to facilitate the men's groups discussing these issues.

5. Include positive masculine values in the definitions of your business values and culture and reinforce positive behaviors and models. ∎

Discussion Questions:

1. Have we labeled the older men in our business as dinosaurs and left them to become extinct? Why?

2. Who is mentoring you on positive masculine values at work? Who are you mentoring?

Outrageous Managers model positive gender roles and values.

Claustrophobia or Creativity

I'm about 6 feet 4 inches tall and I don't fit very well into a box. Actually, I don't know any people who fit well into boxes and yet one of the first things we do when we organize a business is to put all our key players into boxes. The business boxes may be more metaphorical than physical but they are just as confining and uncomfortable. Then we write job descriptions to define the corners of the boxes and squeeze them a little tighter. I get claustrophobic just thinking about this.

Business claustrophobia is a common disease. It originates in the need for specialization but has developed into the need to be able to classify and identify people by their roles. One of the first things we do when we meet someone (at work or elsewhere) is to ask what they do. We can then classify them as accountants, programmers, engineers, manufacturing supervisors or retail clerks. We can also judge them as being at our level or maybe higher or lower. In our supposedly classless society, we have defined clear status levels based on our occupation, level and education. We also pigeonhole people based on these factors and assume that they cannot operate or perform effectively outside of those boundaries. We put them into roles and boxes and discipline them if they escape.

The more we accept our role (or box) in a business, the less of ourselves we bring to work and the more we become disconnected from our passion, our creativity, our inner guidance and our ability to promote or accept learning, change and difference. We eventually become an empty shell of ourselves, robots or the "Stepford Wives" of business. We also become very bored and find other outlets for our passions and ideas. These new outlets can be politics, subterfuge, games, gossip, strict compliance with rules, or other activities at work that can negatively affect the achievement of business goals.

Many executives I have worked with talk about wanting people who can think outside the box. They are looking for creative people who can think and act beyond their roles. Out of the box thinking takes place when we create an atmosphere that encourages people to step out of their narrow roles and feel safe enough to express thoughts freely and openly. We all have creative ideas every day. There is no shortage of creative ideas, only a shortage of businesses willing to hear them and people willing to express them.

Some ideas that may help businesses be less claustrophobic and unlock their creativity:

- Have a creative day every now and then to let people express themselves.

- Have an idea of the day award.

- Throw out your job descriptions and have people write their own talent description.

- Take all the boxes off your organization charts.

- Flatten your organization to the point no one can effectively control anyone else.

- Encourage open communication throughout the business.

- Share leadership on all programs and projects with whoever wants to join in.

- Model creative thinking by taking risks and being willing to appear foolish. ■

Discussion Questions:

1. How do you box your people in? Do you restrict creativity and open expression?

2. Are you a risk taker? When was the last time you intentionally appeared foolish?

Outrageous Managers take risks and have fun.

Chapter 5
Conclusion

Outrageous managers are way cool people. A lot of their traits and characteristics have been defined in this book. This brief chapter summarizes what has been said about them. Outrageous managers have four major qualities and abilities that serve them well and separate them from their peers. They manage the basics of their business. They understand and lead change efforts and actually get them implemented and working. They energize their working relationships and teams. And they are continually working to discover, speak and master the truth.

Outrageous Managers Manage The Basics.

Outrageous Managers achieve outrageous results.

Outrageous Managers use resources wisely.

Outrageous Managers work well with others.
 Outrageous Managers inspire those around them to improve.

Outrageous Managers are continually learning and growing.

Outrageous Managers balance planning, process and performance.

Outrageous Managers ask tough questions.

Outrageous Managers summarize their business plans on one page.

Outrageous Managers build on their past success.

Outrageous Managers get to the root of critical problems and solve them.

Outrageous Managers develop strategies that are consistent with their business culture.

Outrageous Managers organize to serve their customers.

Outrageous Managers put their business plans into action.

Outrageous Managers create community with their customers.

Outrageous Managers master the basics of marketing.

Outrageous Managers use market research to define marketing programs.

Outrageous Managers develop a competitive edge.

Outrageous Managers exercise due diligence on major decisions.

Outrageous Managers align their processes with their business goals.

Outrageous Managers are wildly creative recruiters.

Outrageous Managers hire quickly and wisely.

Outrageous Managers measure performance.

Outrageous Managers demand total accountability.

Outrageous Managers continually improve their financial condition.

Outrageous Managers use simple business decision models.

Outrageous Managers insist on excellent business processes.

Outrageous Managers Lead Change

Outrageous Managers manage simple change.

Outrageous Managers lead transitions.

Outrageous Managers are transformational leaders.

Outrageous Managers are lifelong learners.

Outrageous Managers are passionately involved.

Outrageous Managers are wildly inventive.

Outrageous Managers personify integrity.

Outrageous Managers initiate action.

Outrageous Managers embrace the unknown.

Outrageous Managers lead technology change.

Outrageous Managers are tenacious about implementation.

Outrageous Managers partner with their consultants.

Outrageous Managers kill bureaucracy before it spreads.

Outrageous Managers hate bureaucracy.

Outrageous Managers courageously turn around their business.

Outrageous Managers Energize Their Relationships and Teams

Outrageous Managers attract excellent people.

Outrageous Managers pay attention to their working relationships.

Outrageous Managers openly express their feelings.

Outrageous Managers have a bias for action.

Outrageous Managers develop team commitment.

Outrageous Managers are cooperative.

Outrageous Managers compose diverse teams.

Outrageous Managers measure and reward team contributions.

Outrageous Managers energize their communities.

Outrageous Managers follow their dreams and passions.

Outrageous Managers thrive on differences.

Outrageous Managers create cooperation.

Outrageous Managers are great communicators.

Outrageous Managers celebrate and reward outstanding performance.

Outrageous Managers love and encourage positive conflict.

Outrageous Managers root out and resolve negative conflicts.

Outrageous Managers model effective feedback and coaching.

Outrageous Managers include and invite.

Outrageous Managers Master The Truth

Outrageous Managers know themselves.

Outrageous Managers always speak the truth.

Outrageous Managers earn and nurture trust.

Outrageous Managers are emotionally intelligent.

Outrageous Managers let their imaginations run free.

Outrageous Managers abhor unethical behavior.

Outrageous Managers instill positive business values.

Outrageous Managers nurture creativity and growth.

Outrageous Managers value and use their intuition.

Outrageous Managers embrace social truth.

Outrageous Managers model positive gender roles and values.

Outrageous Managers take risks and have fun.

Outrageous Managers have soul!!! ■

Appendix A
Bibliography of Sources and Readings

Adams, John D, ed. (1984), *Transforming Work*. Miles River Press, Alexandria, VA.

Adams, John D, ed.(1986), *Transforming Leadership*. Miles River Press, Alexandria, VA.

Adler, Mortimer J. (1981), *Six Great Ideas*. Collier Books, New York.

Agor, Weston H, ed. (1989), *Intuition in Organizations*. Sage, Newbury Park, CA.

Argyris, Chris. (1990), *Overcoming Organizational Defenses*. Allyn and Bacon, Boston.

Aronson, Elliot. (1984), *The Social Animal*. 4th ed. W.H. Freeman, New York.

Bee, Helen L. (1987), *The Journey of Adulthood*. Macmillan, New York.

Beckhard, Richard and Reuben T. Harris. (1987), *Organizational Transitions*. Addison-Wesley, Reading, MA.

Bellah, Robert N. et al., eds. (1986), *Habits of The Heart*. Harper and Row, New York.

Bellah, Robert N. et al., eds. (1987), *Individualism and Commitment in American Life*. Harper and Row, New York.

Bennis, Warren. (1989), *Why Leaders Can't Lead*. Jossey-Bass, San Francisco.

Bennis, Warren. (1989), *On Becoming a Leader*. Addison-Wesley, Reading, MA.

Blanchard, Kenneth and Norman Vincent Peale. (1988), *The Power of Ethical Management*. William Morrow, New York.

Block, Peter. (1987), *The Empowered Manager*. Jossey-Bass, San Francisco.

Bolman, Lee G. and Terrence E. Deal. (1984), *Modern Approaches to Understanding and Managing Organizations*. Jossey-Bass, San Francisco.

Appendix A–Bibliography of Sources and Readings

Borisoff, Deborah and David A. Victor. (1989), *Conflict Management*. Prentice-Hall, Englewood Cliffs, NJ.

Bridges, William. (1980), *Transitions*. Addison-Wesley, Reading, MA.

Burke, W. Warner. (1987), *Organization Development*. Addison-Wesley, Reading, MA.

Campbell, Joseph with Bill Moyers. (1988), *The Power Of Myth*. Doubleday, New York.

Capra, Fritjof. (1982), *The Turning Point*. Bantam, New York.

Csikszentmihalyi, Mihaly. (1990), *Flow*. Harper and Row, New York.

Deaux, Kay and Lawrence S Wrightsman. (1988), *Social Psychology*. 5th ed. Brooks /Cole, Pacific Grove, CA.

Dyer, William G. (1987), *Team Building*. 2nd ed. Addison-Wesley, Reading, MA.

Freeman, R. Edward and Daniel R. Gilbert Jr. (1988), *Corporate Strategy And The Search For Ethics*. Prentice Hall, Englewood Cliffs, NJ.

Frost, Peter J. et al., eds. (1985), *Organizational Culture*. Sage, Newbury Park, CA.

Goleman, Daniel. (1995), *Emotional Intelligence*. Bantam Books, New York.

Grof, Stanislav and Christina Grof, eds. (1989), *Spiritual Emergency*. Jeremy P. Tarcher, Los Angeles.

Hawley, Jack. (1993), *Reawakening The Spirit In Work*. Simon and Schuster, New York.

Hickman, Craig R. and Michael A.Silva. (1984), *Creating Excellence*. New American Library, New York.

Horan, Jim. (1997), *The One Page Business Plan*. Rent.a.CFO, El Sobrante, CA.

Huang, Chungliang Al and Jerry Lynch. (1995), *Mentoring*. Harper, San Francisco.

Huxley, Aldous. (1944), *The Perennial Philosophy*. Harper and Row, New York.

Kanter, Rosabeth Moss. (1983), *The Change Masters*. Simon and Schuster, New York.

Katzenbach, Jon R and Douglas K Smith. (1993), *The Wisdom Of Teams*. Harper Business, New York, NY.

Kelman, Herbert C. and V. Lee Hamilton. (1989), *Crimes of Obedience*. Yale University Press, New Haven CT.

Kilmann, Ralph H. et al. (1985), *Gaining Control Of The Corporate Culture*. Jossey-Bass, San Francisco.

McWhinney, Will. (1991), *Paths of Change*. Sage, Beverly Hills, CA.

Morgan, Gareth. (1986), *Images of Organization*. Sage, Beverly Hills, CA.

Morgan, Gareth. (1988), *Riding The Waves Of Change*. Jossey-Bass, San Francisco.

Peters, Thomas J. and Robert H. Waterman Jr. (1982), *In Search Of Excellence*. Harper and Row, New York.

Peters, Tom and Nancy Austin. (1985), *A Passion for Excellence*. Warner, New York.

Peters, Tom. (1987), *Thriving On Chaos*. Alfred A. Knopf, New York.

Quinn, Robert E. (1988), *Beyond Rational Management*. Jossey-Bass, San Francisco.

Ray, Michael and Rochelle Myers. (1986), *Creativity in Business*. Doubleday, New York.

Ray, Michael and Alan Rinzler, eds. (1993), *The New Paradigm In Business*. Jeremy P. Tarcher, Los Angeles.

Reddy, W. Brendan, ed. (1988), *Team Building*. NTL Institute and University Associates, Alexandria, VA and San Diego, CA.

Rogers, Carl R. (1961), *On Becoming A Person*. Houghton Mifflin, Boston.

Schein, Edgar H. (1980), *Organizational Psychology*. 3rd ed. Prentice-Hall, Englewood Cliffs, NJ.

Schein, Edgar H. (1985), *Organizational Culture and Leadership*. Jossey-Bass, San Francisco.

Schon, Donald A. (1983), *The Reflective Practitioner*. Basic Books, New York.

Scott, Gini Graham. (1990), *Resolving Conflict*. New Harbinger, Oakland, CA.

Senge, Peter M. (1990), *The Fifth Discipline*. Doubleday, New York.

Srivastva, Suresh and Assoc., eds. (1983), *The Executive Mind*. Jossey-Bass, San Francisco.

Stokes, Kenneth, ed. (1982), *Faith Development in the Adult Lifecycle*. W.H. Sadlier, New York.

Vail, Peter B. (1989), *Managing As A Performing Art*. Jossey-Bass, San Francisco.

Vaughan, Frances E. (1979), *Awakening Intuition*. Doubleday, New York.

Walsh, Roger N. and Frances Vaughan, eds. (1980), *Beyond Ego*. Jeremy P. Tarcher, Los Angeles.

Weeks, Dudley. (1992), *The Eight Essential Steps To Conflict Resolution*. Jeremy P. Tarcher, Los Angeles.

Wheatley, Margaret J. (1992), *Leadership and the New Science*. Berrett-Koehler, San Francisco.

Wilber, Ken. (1977), *The Spectrum of Consciousness*. Theosophical Publishing House, Wheaton, IL.

Appendix B

How To Use This Book

*T*his book is designed to be used in many ways. The number of uses is limited only by our imagination. It can be used as an ongoing program for individuals, managers and teams, or as a reference, a one year program or a learning guide. This book explores several business topics. The general outline is to discuss a few brief cases on each topic, to share some wisdom gained over thirty years of managing and consulting on the issues and then to ask discussion questions. This book explores the essence of the topics. It does not try to cover all the topics or to cover each in depth. The purpose is to introduce the topics in articles that can be read in under five minutes and then to ask the questions that will encourage exploration and applications of the topics to your business or organization.

The discussion of applications of the topics to your business or organization is the true value of using this book. A few suggested ways to maximize the benefits are outlined below. Please pick the ways that work best for you or invent your own ways. The discussions and the implementation are the keys whichever method you use.

You can use this book to:

1. Develop your management teams in weekly meetings.

2. Focus weekly staff meetings.

3. Provide the focus for management retreats.

4. Outline workshops on many of the book's topics.

5. Train and develop your managers in a class-room.

6. Be part of a self directed learning program.

7. Set expectations and goals for your managers and team leaders.

8. Focus your planning team.

9. Focus change efforts.

10. Define and implement leadership development programs.

11. Define and implement team development programs.

12. Create and implement programs on organization ethics.

13. Energize your organization and your people.

14. Improve your performance.

15. Set policies for how you want to manage and lead your organization. ■